From Learners to Leaders

Purchases of AASL publications and products fund advocacy, leadership, professional development, and standards initiatives for school librarians nationally.

ALA Editions purchases fund advocacy, awareness, and accreditation programs for library professionals worldwide.

From Learners to Leaders

Empowering Student Volunteers in the School Library

Dione Mila and Diana Haneski

CHICAGO | 2025

Dione Mila is a public elementary school librarian in South Florida, the first in Broward County to earn the coveted Florida Power-Library School Award. She has served as president of the Broward County Association of Media Specialists, Region 5, chair for the Florida Association for Media in Education, and chair for the Sunshine State Young Readers Award program, Grades 3–5; and is a frequent speaker at FAME Conferences. Her experience, research, and application of learner leadership in the school library allows her to present at local, state, and national conferences, inspiring others to incorporate learner leadership within their own school libraries.

Diana Haneski is the National Board–certified educator/librarian at Marjory Stoneman Douglas High School, a Florida Power-Library School in Parkland, Florida. Her work with learner leaders at Westglades Middle, Park Trails Elementary, and Silver Lakes Elementary Schools motivates her to mentor new librarians and explore ways to create joyful library programs. A 2024 recipient of ALA's I Love My Librarian Award, she loves to help readers find books that interest them and works hard to create a welcoming environment at the library. Along with her therapy dog, River, she speaks at conferences on how library workers can find joy by offering engaging programs, updating library spaces, and supporting their communities' mental health.

ISBN: 979-8-89255-329-2 (paper)

Library of Congress Cataloging-in-Publication Data

Names: Mila, Dione author | Haneski, Diana author

Title: From learners to leaders : empowering student volunteers in the school library / Dione Mila and Diana Haneski.

Description: Chicago : ALA Editions, 2025. | Includes bibliographical references and index.

Identifiers: LCCN 2025011819 | ISBN 9798892553292 paperback

Subjects: LCSH: Student volunteers in libraries | Leadership—Study and teaching | School libraries

Classification: LCC Z682.4.V64 M55 2025 | DDC 023—dc23/eng/20250616

LC record available at https://lccn.loc.gov/2025011819

Book design by Alejandra Diaz in the Galano Classic, Utopia Std, and Source Sans typefaces.

♾ This paper meets the requirements of ANSI/NISO Z39.48-1992 (Permanence of Paper).

Printed in the United States of America

29 28 27 26 25 5 4 3 2 1

To all our learners, past and present,
whose dedication, heart, and creativity have enriched
our library programs beyond measure.

WEB EXTRAS: Sample materials from part II can be downloaded at **alaeditions.org/AASLextras.**

CONTENTS

PREFACE

From Author Dione Mila

Walking into my first role as the librarian at a public elementary school, I remember the excitement and desire to bring new ideas to the space. A touch of paint here, some new shelving, some eye-catching signage?

Oh, who am I kidding? I didn't have a clue.

After seven years as a classroom educator, I started my library role by creating colossal standards-based lesson plans for each grade level. Then, the reality of nine or ten, 30-minute daily classes, with 20 to 30 learners in each class—and sometimes double classes—coming into the library came crashing down on me! By the time a class finished a book check-out and went out the door, the next class was already waiting for me. Where were the standards-based lessons? How would I manage teaching library skills and information literacy, checking out books, putting all the books back on the shelf, and instilling excitement for reading? With no clerk, few parents for support, and a list of must-dos a mile long, I could barely breathe. Oh, and then came the responsibility for the morning news program—and yes, I needed to learn how to work the equipment because it was new and no one knew how to use it. What? I was in way over my head.

Slowly, I was able to spot some trends. Each class had a few learners who liked to help and were willing to learn how to assist with the check-out for their class. Their support freed me to help learners find good-fit books and answer questions. Then, they asked if more help was needed, and the response was "*Yes!*" Relying on their assistance, I soon learned that my learners could help put books back on the book trolley and teach the other learners how to put books back on the trolly—which made reshelving much easier—along with a variety of other tasks! But more remarkable than the immense help they gave me was the learners' pride and self-confidence when completing a task.

The most significant ah-ha moment came when visiting my daughter at the Air Force Academy, where she had just survived her grueling summer boot camp and was starting her first semester. Watching the seniors take command and train the freshman in all aspects of college life at the academy, I thought, "Why not in my elementary school, too?"

The concept emerged: learners taking the lead in running their school library space and teaching their peers. Our morning news program now has directors who have learned the technology side of running a broadcast. During the last month of school, these leaders teach the following year's directors all the ins and outs of running the news. Our fifth-grade learner anchors write the scripts, gathering the weather forecast, lunch menu, and any noteworthy news for that day's broadcast. After one week of being live on the ITE News, they are the pros and must begin teaching the next round of anchors. Each group trains the next group. I've had learners who were petrified to go in front of the camera that first day, but by the end of their two-week period, they were outgoing, knowledgeable, and self-confident. Most importantly, they were eager to train the incoming anchors, and their faces and demeanor showed their pride.

Our Library Teachers of Tomorrow (TOTs) program is a testament to the empowerment of learners. The outgoing fourth-grade TOTs take the "Newbies"—the third-graders who will be in fourth grade next year—under their wing and proudly show them the ropes. There's nothing more satisfying than seeing the learners take ownership of their roles and teach the incoming learners everything they know and value in their job titles. The "Newbies No More" then start their fourth-grade year ready to help learners check their books in and out, reshelve books, create bookmarks, set up and run makerspace stations, and create book displays. And every year, they come up with new ideas to make our library even better than it already is.

While the transformation didn't happen overnight, it did happen, and it was highly effective. As a new mother, I had relied on principles from the Systematic Training for Effective Parenting class to communicate effectively and understand my young children's mindsets. This course profoundly impacted how my husband and I raised our children, encouraging us to view situations from their perspective and provide opportunities for their growth and self-development. Using these principles in the classroom worked wonders, so why not in the library?

Reading the publication of *The One Minute Manager* by Kenneth Blanchard and Spencer Johnson (1982) cemented my belief that learners need to be leaders in our schools and in the library. This happens by gradually releasing responsibility to learners to foster a sense of ownership and pride in their tasks. Age-appropriate responsibilities—such as helping scan the books for return, setting up table displays, and teaching other learners how to use a makerspace center—came to mind when looking for opportunities for learners to assist in the library. Now a fourth-grade leadership crew called Media TOTs runs the library every morning. The fifth-grade ITE News program is run entirely by learners with little to no intervention on my part. Starting small, the Library Leaders program blossomed into a fully functioning, learner-led one.

After sharing this program with my district during our monthly meetings and with state peers at our annual conference, many librarians began contacting me personally to tell me of their own library leadership program success! Each tweaked the original documents to suit their needs, and the results were spectacular. You, too, can tap into your learners' potential, allowing them to grow and become an integral part of your school library culture. Remember, it's a gradual process, but the results are worth it.

—**D. M.**

From Author Diana Haneski

Before being hired as a library media specialist, I would ponder possibilities for lessons and activities and wonder, "How will I fill the time in a school day teaching learners? What if I run out of ideas?" But once I started my first position at Silver Lakes Elementary (SLE), I quickly learned how exciting and engaging a school library career could be. Suddenly, with wide-eyed wonder, I thought, "Wow, there are so many possibilities." I went to school every day, inspired and bursting with ideas.

The school enrolled nearly a thousand learners, and between the huge number of learners visiting our beautiful space, the vast array of books, and all the plans and resources, things soon began to pile up. Our kind, eager-to-help clerk and I needed to organize the chaos I'd created, and thankfully, parents in the school community offered to help. I also welcomed help from my young sons, Carey and Kyle, who attended school with me at SLE. If they were not reading or doing their homework in the library, I put them to work with my husband Ray, who volunteered in the afternoons. I always asked my volunteers what job they wanted to do, and it proved to be a successful strategy—the more they liked the job, the more pride they put into it. I quickly learned that parents are a key to getting things done in any school library. Wanting to be with their kids after school, many parents joined their children in the library to lend an extra set of hands. Suddenly, I had help from all ages. I delighted in the lively buzz of chatter and laughter as we worked to make the best program possible.

From those early days, I learned the value of delegating. The willingness of volunteers to help me during my early years in the profession kept me motivated, and like the little engine that could, my mantra was "I think I can. I think I can!" I didn't shed tears as I thought I might. Later, while at Westglades Middle, I had three generations from one family that came in to help in our school library. The grandmother continued to help me when I moved to Marjory Stoneman Douglas High School. I have much gratitude for these families over the years, and I learned from watching these parents and grandparents guide their children to success. These are some of my best memories of working at a school.

I produced the live daily TV announcements program for seventeen years. This additional task was like having an extra class in the morning before school even began. Fortunately, my previous profession was in broadcasting, so I had a good idea of what needed to happen. I found learners who liked to act and be in front of the camera and some who loved technology and gadgets, and soon, we were *live*. The learners worked quickly, gave their best, and demonstrated a good attitude. Naturally, they stepped up to help each other, especially when the clock was ticking. They knew they needed to be ready. Once we produced our first broadcast, I wondered how to keep the momentum going. How do I get more young broadcasters to sign up—then and for future school years? The answers are in the pages ahead.

Learner leaders need direction, and that takes time away from the circulation desk or from working on researching databases with other learners. Educators are often reluctant to delegate to learners or adults, but that's when the magic happens. People who volunteer or young adult learners who want service hours want to help you. Invite them in, take the time to give them an orientation, tell them you will be there to guide and assist, let go of feeling you have to do it all yourself, and watch your library program blossom. I learned early on that help is needed and the time spent training volunteers is worth it. I love when someone comes in thinking they might want to help. I welcome them, tell them I will point them in the direction they are interested in, and let them shine. I have become comfortable delegating responsibilities to my learners, leaders, helpers, and volunteers—a skill that's led to a better library program.

At our high school, we encouraged learners to read Sean Covey's *7 Habits of Highly Effective Teens* (1998), and specifically habit 1, "To Be proactive." A book that helped me understand learners better, *Mindset: The New Psychology of Success* by Carol S. Dweck (2006), supports both the trainee and the trainer to be effective leaders, have a growth mindset, meet challenges, and succeed academically. Our educators utilize the resources in the Leader in Me framework from Franklin Covey Education to nurture learner leadership and boost academic success in learners. Now, it is just like my early days with families. I embrace the incredible kindness and delight in the laughter of the young adult learner leaders as they work. We talk about books, information literacy, technology, and more, and we get the work done proudly, with much heart.

You can read on to get all you need for a learner leadership program.

—D. H.

ACKNOWLEDGMENTS

Nothing good comes without struggle and triumph, so first I would like to thank Diana Haneski for taking this journey with me. Thank you to our incredible editors, Jamie and Stephanie, for their enthusiasm, guidance, and words of wisdom. Thank you to AASL and ALA Editions for believing in the dream of spreading this message to more school libraries. Throughout this career in education, there have been so many inspirational educators and librarians who have each played their role—thank you. A deep and heartfelt thank-you to Miranda and Matt, who inspire me every day, and to my husband, Paul, whose unwavering belief in me and gentle encouragement always pushes me to excel.

—DIONE MILA

Big love to all the librarians who create diverse, essential programs and a safe haven for all. Thank you to my learners and families who support school libraries. Dione Mila, your encouragement to pursue a mutual goal helped this project come to fruition. Jean Anders, you make everything better. Elaine Aaron, your morning phone calls are the best professional development. Thank you to our editors, Jamie and Stephanie, who sparked enthusiasm for writing and encouraged us on this journey.

I am grateful for my husband, Ray Haneski, and sons, Carey and Kyle—they make it joyful and prove love is the answer. Grazie to my parents, Santo and Mariangela, who lived by the motto "If you make someone happy, you'll be happy too."

—DIANA HANESKI

INTRODUCTION

The seed for this book was sown many years ago, when we discovered an opportunity to provide real-world experiences for our learners to build their skill base and provide much-needed confidence.

We have come together to share all the necessary methods and tools to empower your learners as library leaders and achieve the school library you hope for.

The benefits of creating your own group of student volunteers as library leaders are vast. From building strong leadership skills in your learners, to providing more time for the school librarian to focus on high-priority needs of the library, to creating a dynamic and welcoming school library space, our learner leadership program offers a pathway to synergistically encompass the *National School Library Standards for Learners, School Librarians, and School Libraries.*

To help you get started, this book includes:

- easy-to-follow goal-setting and task lists
- clear instructions on building your leadership team
- example forms and templates
- anecdotes to help you visualize success
- training ideas and time frames
- examples of effective modeling, problem-solving, accountability, and self-reflection
- positive redirection methods for effective behavior management
- checkpoints to help guarantee your successful leadership program

Each chapter wraps up with a Putting It into Perspective section, which shows how the principles are put into practice and summarizes what you have learned.

We hope to motivate and inspire with anecdotes and strategies that span the levels from primary through secondary and beyond and to share ideas that you can incorporate into your own stellar school library leadership program. Read on to discover how you can develop your student volunteers from learners to leaders who manage their school library and support their learning community.

PART I

Building Learner-Led Success in the School Library

1

The Benefits of Library Leadership

When school librarians empower learners to take the lead in managing the school library space and working with their peers, they open up numerous opportunities for growth, benefiting both the library and the wider learning community. Learner leadership in the school library brings a variety of advantages for students, school librarians, and the libraries themselves. For learners, it enhances collaboration and communication via teamwork activities, fosters critical thinking and problem-solving through active engagement and Socratic methods, encourages creativity and resilience as their confidence builds, and promotes inclusivity and respect by strengthening community connections. School librarians benefit from the invaluable gift of time, allowing them to focus on high-priority tasks and responsibilities in their roles as leader, instructional partner, information specialist, teacher, and program administrator. Through these roles, school librarians demonstrate and uphold the AASL Common Beliefs of the profession as fundamental to effective school libraries. A library leadership program not only enables you to build essential skills in your library leaders through the Shared Foundations but also allows you to enact these fundamental principles aligning with the *National School Library Standards for Learners, School Librarians, and School Libraries.* A learner-led school library gains greater visibility within the school community and promotes a welcoming space that emphasizes engagement, inclusion, and thoughtful planning for a robust and thriving learning environment.

Benefits to Learners

Learners who take on leadership roles in the school library gain valuable real-world experiences that will help them throughout their school years and beyond. Empowering our learners to lead builds competency in four key areas: collaboration and communication, critical thinking and problem-solving, creativity and resilience, and inclusivity and respect. By providing age-appropriate small tasks in the library, school librarians can create opportunities for learners to take on leadership roles and responsibilities, thereby developing these essential skills and fostering independence and confidence in their abilities.

Collaboration and Communication

One significant benefit of a leadership program is that it helps learners build strong connections with each other and with other school library users. Developing relationships with peers, mentors, and the wider community fosters a sense of belonging and mutual support. These connections enhance collaboration, communication skills, and the ability to work effectively in a team setting. For example, in a library leadership program, learners frequently collaborate on projects, share responsibilities, and support each other in achieving common goals.[1] This experience not only strengthens their interpersonal skills but also creates a network of supportive relationships that can last a lifetime.

The morning news program at Dione's elementary school is a collaborative effort of fifth-graders who work to produce a daily program that is broadcast live to the entire school and beyond, to the local community. The fifth-grade directors lead the charge as they usher in the rotating two-week anchors; this means that each fifth-grade educator selects four learners to appear live for two weeks. From Wednesday to Friday, the previous news anchors show the new anchors how to write scripts, work the camera, act as the weatherperson, and alert the school community that the live broadcast is starting using the all-call system, ensuring that the new anchors are ready to go solo on Monday.

Coming into the newsroom at 7:20 a.m., before the school day has begun, the directors and anchors work together to guarantee the script is written, the daily-announcement transitions are created, the birthday announcements are loaded, the "Day in History" segment is recorded, the weather report is loaded, and the microphones are checked. The directors need to work the news equipment, the soundboard, and the laptop. They oversee the news anchors and keep those learners on track in a professional manner. This method of giving these learners ownership of their daily news program allows them to work with a variety of other learners, all working toward a common goal of creating and curating a daily news broadcast that informs and motivates our school community.[2]

Critical Thinking and Problem-Solving

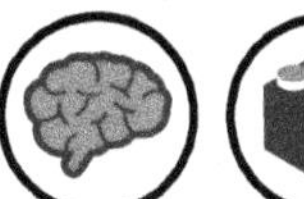

Library leadership programs promote strong critical thinking and problem-solving skills. Nurture these skills and provide opportunities for development. By encouraging learners' confidence in their emerging skills, school librarians foster a safe and supportive learning environment that builds critical thinking and problem-solving temperaments for all learners.[3]

At Dione's elementary school, library leaders often become flustered when first learning to use the library's online card catalog and management system. When the computer doesn't do what they want, they often turn to the school librarian and exclaim, "It doesn't work." With an inward chuckle, Dione asks her befuddled leaders, "Okay, but how would I solve that? What seems to be the disconnect?" As the learners go through the steps they took to arrive at their current problem, many times they realize their mistake and sheepishly grin. "I knew you could solve that!" Dione exclaims as she gives that leader a huge smile. She then helps the learner realize that giving up at the first hurdle isn't helpful for anyone. Instead, look for any errors that could have caused the problem. Then work backward to find the solution. Building their personal belief in their critical thinking resiliency is a key step in nurturing strong problem-solving skills.[4]

Creativity and Resilience

Another benefit of a leadership program is that it nurtures creativity in learners. Encouraging learners to think creatively and explore new ideas fosters confidence and self-expression. When individuals feel confident in their creative abilities, they're more likely to take risks, innovate, and solve problems effectively.[5] This environment of creativity not only enhances personal growth but also contributes to a vibrant and dynamic community.

For example, in both our elementary and high school library leadership programs, learners are asked for their input when renovating and updating library spaces. They are shown color, fabric, style, and design options, and opinions are encouraged. They brainstormed, collaborated, and came up with a theme that included vibrant murals, cozy reading nooks, and interactive displays. In this task, library leaders worked together to create a fun and festive school library space. The leaders discussed various ideas, decided how they wanted the space to look, and were off accomplishing their plan. These learners took ownership of the school library space and enjoyed the comments and compliments from their peers who walked into the school library. This project showcased the learners' creativity while instilling a sense of pride and ownership in their work, boosting their confidence and reinforcing the importance of self-expression.

Inclusivity and Respect

Library leadership programs powerfully promote inclusivity and respect. By encouraging diverse voices and perspectives, these programs create an environment where everyone feels valued and heard. Inclusivity fosters a sense of belonging and community, which in turn nurtures mutual respect among learners. When students from different backgrounds collaborate and share their unique experiences, they develop a deeper understanding and appreciation for each other. This strengthens the community and prepares learners to thrive in a diverse world. Library leadership is a beacon of unity, demonstrating that respect and inclusivity are fundamental to personal and collective growth.[6]

Through fostering a welcoming school library, library leaders build empathy for others. Students and educators enter a school library for many reasons, including a desire to feel like they belong. As your library leaders lead, by helping peers with book recommendations, conducting mini library tours, and welcoming new learners to your school library, they learn that everyone has value.

Once learners understand that everyone and their range of perspectives has value, this is a perfect opportunity to also build learners' respect when engaging with others, with various ideas, and when sharing information in the wider world.[7] Library leaders often model safe and ethical use of tools and technologies with library users, and in doing so demonstrate responsible and respectful behavior when sharing information and ideas.

Benefits to School Librarians

Implementing a library leadership program allows school librarians to deepen their engagement with the five key roles of the school librarian: leader, instructional partner, teacher, information specialist, and program administrator.[8] As a *leader*, school librarians can inspire and guide learner leaders, fostering a collaborative and dynamic school library environment. In the role of *instructional partner*, the librarian facilitates a leadership program that promotes more-effective collaboration with other educators, enriching the curriculum with diverse resources and innovative teaching strategies. As a *teacher*, school librarians can focus on delivering high-quality instruction, knowing they have support for managing the daily operations of the school library. The role of *information specialist* is elevated through the delegation of routine tasks to learner leaders, allowing school librarians to concentrate on curating and providing access to essential information and resources. Finally, as a *program administrator*, school librarians can streamline administrative tasks and develop more-impactful programs, supported by the reliable assistance of learner leaders. This holistic approach not only enhances the school librarian's ability to fulfill their own critical roles but also empowers learners as leaders in creating a vibrant and inclusive school library community.

Leader

School librarians as leaders can motivate and mentor student leaders by offering opportunities for learners to get involved and take on responsibilities. By engaging learners in meaningful projects and decision-making processes, school librarians demonstrate the value of leadership and teamwork. This empowers learners; it also cultivates their sense of ownership and pride in the school library.

For example, school librarians can assign learner leaders to manage specific sections of the library, organize events, or lead book clubs. Through these activities, learners develop critical skills such as communication, problem-solving, and collaboration. Additionally, leaders can serve as role models for their peers, promoting a culture of mutual respect and support. This collaborative approach transforms the school library into a vibrant learning hub where both learners and school librarians thrive.

Instructional Partner

School librarians play a crucial role in enriching the curriculum through their collaboration with other educators. By actively working with classroom and content-area educators, school librarians can integrate a wealth of diverse resources into the learning experience, making the curriculum more engaging and effective.

For example, school librarians can provide educators with access to a broad range of multimedia materials, databases, and specialized collections that align with various subjects being taught. The library leadership team can then be tasked with supplying additional support for the educator and to their peers.

The school librarian can also introduce innovative teaching methods such as inquiry-based learning, project-based assignments, and digital literacy skills, which help enhance learners' critical thinking and problem-solving abilities. This collaboration ensures that educators have the tools and support they need to deliver high-quality instruction, ultimately benefiting learning outcomes.

Teacher

School librarians can prioritize delivering high-quality instruction, confident that they have support for handling daily operations. With the assistance of learner leaders or library aides managing routine tasks such as shelving books, organizing materials, and overseeing check-outs, school librarians can dedicate more time to instructional activities. This includes conducting engaging library lessons, providing research guidance, and integrating information literacy into the curriculum. By delegating administrative responsibilities, school librarians can focus on crafting impactful learning experiences, thereby enhancing the overall educational environment. Additionally, this support system allows school librarians to stay current with new instructional strategies and resources, further enriching the educational experiences they provide.

Information Specialist

By delegating routine tasks to library leaders, school librarians can enhance their role as information specialists, focusing on curating and providing access to crucial information and resources. This shift allows school librarians to identify and acquire relevant materials that support the curriculum, ensuring that learners and educators have access to the latest and most pertinent information.

For instance, instead of spending time on routine tasks, school librarians can dedicate their efforts to evaluating and selecting new books, databases, and digital resources that align with the needs and interests of the school community. They can also create specialized collections, such as those focused on STEM, diversity, or local history, which can enrich the learning experience. Additionally, school librarians can develop and deliver training sessions for learners and staff on how to effectively use these resources, thereby enhancing the overall information literacy of the school community. Moreover, library leaders are often trained to help deliver these training sessions or record assistance modules for various tech resources, fostering a collaborative learning environment and empowering other learners to take on active roles in their educational journey.

By focusing on these high-impact activities, school librarians not only improve the quality and accessibility of the library's resources but also reinforce their role as essential information specialists within the educational ecosystem.

Program Administrator

School librarians can optimize administrative processes through the library leadership program and create more powerful school libraries. High-priority tasks such as inventory, monthly newsletters, and writing grants can present valuable opportunities for library leaders to take on and share responsibilities, allowing the school librarian time to focus on other equally high-priority tasks that require time for careful reflection.

Inventory can be a shared task among several library leaders as each is trained on how to scan books into the inventory database. The school library newsletter is a key advocacy tool, but why spend hours creating stories and infographics for your monthly newsletter when your library leaders can create inspiring stories and eye-catching graphics? Daily announcements are also an area for library leaders to take ownership and support the school library. Looking to increase your budget through grants such as DonorsChoose? Library leaders can help facilitate the photographs and thank-you letters to fulfill the obligations associated with grants. Each shared task allows the school librarian to focus on future projects and benefits to the library, creating a dynamic and engaging space for the learners and the school community.

Gaining the freedom to assess the current collection and devise plans for improvement is crucial as school librarians develop and uphold collection development strategies. Years ago, Dione spent countless weekends on data and writing the 30-page collection development plan. Now, with library leaders on board and freeing up more time, meeting with the library advisory committee is a joy, celebrating achievements. And Dione's weekends? They're finally hers.

Program administration is a vital responsibility among a school librarian's roles. Program administration involves managing the school library's resources, facilities, and budget to ensure they align with the educational goals of the school. This includes developing and maintaining collection development plans, creating policies that support effective school library operations, and overseeing the implementation of these policies. By efficiently organizing and coordinating various library activities, school librarians can provide a well-structured and dynamic learning environment. Additionally, strong program administration enables school librarians to identify and respond to the needs of learners and staff, ensuring that the school library remains a pivotal resource for the learning community.

Implementing a library leadership program in the school library allows the school librarian to focus on building their strengths in their five key roles. Remember, every step forward brings you closer to these well-deserved benefits!

Benefits to School Libraries

Not only do learners and school librarians benefit from library leadership programs, but the school library flourishes with these efforts. By aligning your library leadership program with the six Common Beliefs of the school library profession,[9] you can create a strategic and organized approach to growing your school library and enhancing opportunities for your learning community. Library leaders allow you time to focus on bringing to life these Common Beliefs that are fundamentally important to school libraries.

Common Belief 1: The school library is a unique and essential part of a learning community.

Every learner wants to feel welcome at their school library. The school library is a central learning hub that fosters engagement and community, providing neutral ground for conversation and equitable access to opportunities for all. These elements make the school library unique and essential when planning welcoming spaces for learning to take place.

Providing learner engagement, inclusion, respect, and thoughtful consideration to space planning and signage all create a sense of belonging in your school library. It's important to give voice to your library leaders as they help you create the school library every learner deserves.

Fostering Learner Engagement

When learners enter the school library, they're looking for a place where they belong. Does your school library create that welcoming atmosphere? Learners come with different levels of library experience. Some need basic guidance; others can assist classmates. Acknowledging and utilizing eager helpers, especially during busy periods, minimizes confusion and fosters a supportive environment. If learners are unsure about finding a book, locating library sections, or navigating check-out procedures, they should feel comfortable seeking answers. Foster a supportive environment where helping each other is encouraged and asking for help is met with understanding rather than judgment.

Effective Space Planning

Whether you have been given a substantial grant, a district refresh, or community support, creating a visually stimulating, updated, and inviting space is essential to a school library. Share space plans and choices of furnishings with your library leaders to gather their opinions and gain their support.

For example, when choosing colors for her new rocking chairs, Dione put out all the color samples from the vendor and asked learners to choose up to five colors. Educators, families, and learners all gave their thoughtful notions of the perfect combination. Now each colorful and curvy table has its own color of rocking chairs for learners to enjoy during their lessons, and Dione has a much easier way to designate small groups with the learners: by chair color.

Thoughtful Signage

Signage is an important vehicle to drive circulation and ease of use for your library patrons. Do your library leaders use a graphics platform such as Canva or Adobe Express? Have them create engaging displays and signs. Do you have parent volunteers with hidden artistic talents? Employ them to craft promotions for monthly displays and guide your library learners. Do you have an artistic learner who can create real artwork in your school library to guide others to find needed resources? Allow their talent to brighten your space.

Diana has long held a goal for her leaders to create the signage for genres, book displays, upcoming events, and other library programming. After many years of modeling and occasional frustrations, her dreams became reality. Recognizing her clerk's enthusiasm for an online graphic design tool, Diana encouraged collaboration between the clerk and the leaders to create eye-catching graphics. These vibrant signs are now displayed throughout the library, guiding users to favorite books, new resources, and opportunities.

This is where your library leadership program will sparkle and showcase your school library as a unique and essential part of the learning community, providing all learners with opportunities for success as they prepare for college, career, and life.

Common Belief 2: Qualified school librarians lead effective school libraries.

School librarians serve as instructional leaders, program administrators, educators, collaborative partners, and information specialists. Qualified school librarians model the effective use of resources and research skills, cultivate an inquiry mindset across the learning community, and create a hub for learning that is available on demand.

With all the positive outcomes of having a learner-led library leadership program, your administration will undoubtedly reap the benefits and support you in your school library. Every administrator wants to shine among their peers at district meetings and when school board members visit their school. Even future parents who visit the school are evaluating the benefits of purchasing a home in your school's zone versus the school down the street. Share the accomplishments of your school library leadership program and those of its learner leaders. Promote its seamless integration with your school's goals through weekly briefings or frequent emails with your administrator. Better yet, invite your administrator to visit the school library, observe your leaders in action, and relish its success.

Common Belief 3: Learners should be prepared for college, career, and life.

The school library improves all learners' opportunities for achievement. "This success empowers learners to persist in inquiry, advanced study, enriching professional work, and community participation through continuous improvement within and beyond the school building and school day."[10]

Learner leaders play a pivotal role in realizing this Common Belief in our school libraries. They champion the growth of resources, fostering an environment where all learners can explore future opportunities. Through initiatives like bringing in diverse speakers, organizing events such as career days, and introducing informative applications, learner leaders help guide and inspire their peers.

Each learner possesses a unique skill set and aspirations, and the school library serves as a safe haven for open discussions about future possibilities. Whether it's academic-centered higher education, technical trade schools, military endeavors, or other passion-driven projects, the school library, with the support of library leaders, encourages every learner to discover and pursue their own path.

Common Belief 4: Reading is the core of personal and academic competency.

The curated school library engages the community through print and digital content to develop lifelong learners and readers. Reading initiatives and a vibrant collection motivate and develop a culture of reading; developing a culture of reading is a top priority for school libraries, and many of the clubs or events a school library would host are reading-centric. As your library leadership program grows and learners take on more responsibilities, the school librarian may find that learner-led extracurricular programs that promote reading and skill development are more attainable.

Book Clubs

Book clubs are after-school activities that can be learner-led or facilitated by parent volunteers. Dione's weekly book club is based off the feedback from a participant survey distributed at the beginning of the year. Learners and families submit their preferences for how often they want to meet, what books they want to read, and how much they wish to read for each meeting. Parent volunteers are welcomed for their participation in staying after school and providing a healthy snack for the participants. Through the Remind app, pictures and important information are shared with the families.

Book Battles

A strong motivational reading club is the book battle. Some school librarians foster in-house grade-level battles, while others are involved in district-wide competitions. At Diana's school, the book club preps for the spring Battle of the Books, meeting twice monthly to discuss one of fifteen state-listed books. Led by the club president and two English language arts educators, learners set goals and get ready for the competition. Throughout the year, library leaders handle event prep, signage, activities, and setup, and inspire other district schools to involve their learners as well.

Other Clubs

Book clubs, book battles, and One Book/One School initiatives are obvious choices for promoting a reading culture, but other clubs may also be considered. Club themes such as manga and anime, poetry, debate, and even gaming—think Minecraft or board-game nights for the community—involve reading and literacy-skill development. If the library leadership program has increased the capacity for the school library to engage in more extracurricular programs, then that opens many doors to further develop a culture of reading and uphold this value central to the profession. Ponder the needs of the learners in your school as well as the local community's needs. Learners may even approach you with a proposal for a new club aimed at attracting the community to your library.

Common Belief 5: Intellectual freedom is every learner's right.

Every school librarian strives to curate an engaging, inclusive, and equitable collection for their learners. Why is having a vibrant collection important? So that when learners exercise their intellectual freedom, they have access to a collection that is up to date, reflective of the community, and inclusive of the larger world. Learners need equitable access to quality information to support their intellectual endeavors and to form their own opinions while being respectful of others' opinions. Focus on providing a safe space for intellectual freedom to flourish, developing the empathy in learners to share ideas; meanwhile, engage your library leaders in activities to help you grow and maintain a vibrant collection!

New Acquisitions

Letting library leaders suggest new purchases gives them a sense of ownership. Provide vendor catalogs and have them find books to fill collection gaps while considering criteria like professional reviews and copyright dates. Create a suggestion box where learners can submit book requests. Supply sticky notes, pencils, and trade magazines at the station, making it easy for learners to mark pages with desired books and turning it into an interactive and learner-driven book recommendation center. Their choices may surprise you, resulting in a list of high-interest books. Watch their excitement as they unpack, process, and display their selections—if any make it to the display before being checked out!

Weeding

Weeding is an area where library leaders truly shine. Pull reports on the collection's age and identify books with outdated copyright dates. Turn it into a game to see who can find the most books listed on the report. Each learner gathers and evaluates the condition, contents, and age of the books, and considers a newer publication. The learners' opinions matter, leading to a thorough investigation before making any weeding decisions. This responsibility fosters ownership and pride in the collection.

Common Belief 6: Information technologies must be appropriately integrated and equitably available.

Equitable access to technology in school libraries bridges digital and socioeconomic divides, ensuring that all learners can build essential skills. Assistive technologies play a crucial role in making information accessible to everyone. Examples of this include providing headphones and other hardware, adaptive tablets or devices, and appropriate applications. These tools are fundamental for creating an inclusive environment where every learner has the opportunity to succeed.

Furthermore, digital ethics is a vital aspect of appropriate technology use. By incorporating infographics and lessons on digital ethics, school libraries can instill this essential life skill in learners. Libraries should also create opportunities for learners to practice and hone their digital citizenship, thereby preparing them for responsible and ethical online behavior.

Library leaders play a pivotal role in facilitating the integration of information technologies and ensuring equitable access. Here are some ways they assist:

- *Creating tutorials and infographics* that educate library users about various digital tools, assistive technologies, and digital ethics. These resources are made available both online and in print, catering to diverse learning preferences.
- *Facilitating training sessions and workshops* for other learners and educators on the effective use of technology. These sessions cover topics such as digital citizenship, cyber safety, and assistive technologies.
- *Providing individual assistance* to library users who may need personalized support with technology. This includes one-on-one sessions to guide them through using specific tools or applications.
- *Encouraging collaborative projects* between learners and educators to create products that utilize technology. This hands-on approach helps learners gain practical experience and confidence in using digital tools.
- *Supporting resource management* to ensure that the school library is equipped with the latest technologies and assistive devices. Library leaders manage the distribution and maintenance of these resources, making sure tools are available and accessible to all library users.

By taking these steps, library leaders not only support the technological needs of the school community but also foster an inclusive and ethical digital environment.

Putting It into Perspective

Creating an environment that welcomes learners as library leaders and develops their skills—while also providing the school librarian the gift of time to deeply reflect on the community's needs within their roles—cultivates a dynamic and engaging school library environment. You will meet district expectations and feel proud of your library leaders' successes. Collaborative efforts create a vibrant school library space cherished by all and keep everyone coming back.

Using learner leadership in your school library aligns with the *National School Library Standards*, creating synergy. Encouraging learners to voice ideas, take risks, solve problems, and make decisions fosters inclusiveness and respect in our diverse school community.

NOTES

1. AASL American Association of School Librarians, *National School Library Standards for Learners, School Librarians, and School Libraries*, 2nd ed. (American Library Association, 2026), Collaborate Key Commitment: "Work effectively with others to broaden perspectives and work toward common goals."
2. AASL, *National School Library Standards*, Curate Key Commitment: "Make meaning for oneself and others by collecting, organizing, and sharing resources of personal relevance."
3. AASL, *National School Library Standards*, Inquire Key Commitment: "Build new knowledge by inquiring, thinking critically, identifying problems, and developing strategies for solving problems."
4. AASL, *National School Library Standards*, Explore Key Commitment: "Discover and innovate in a growth mindset developed through experience and reflection."
5. AASL, *National School Library Standards*, Explore Key Commitment.
6. AASL, *National School Library Standards*, Include Key Commitment: "Demonstrate an understanding of and commitment to inclusiveness and respect for diversity in the learning community."
7. AASL, *National School Library Standards*, Engage Key Commitment: "Demonstrate safe, legal, and ethical creating and sharing of knowledge products independently while engaging in a community of practice and an interconnected world."
8. These key roles are explored in "Grounding Principles of the Profession," chapter 1 of AASL, *National School Library Standards*.
9. The six Common Beliefs are found throughout the *National School Library Standards* and explored in detail in chapter 1, "Grounding Principles of the Profession."
10. AASL, "Common Beliefs," National School Library Standards, 2018, standards.aasl.org/beliefs.

2

Getting Started

To effectively implement learner leadership programs in your school library, begin by identifying leadership opportunities and finding your team. To build a cohesive team, you'll need to identify and assess needs and roles, gather candidates, screen and select participants, and obtain necessary permissions. These foundational steps will set the stage for a program that empowers learners and enhances your school library's role within the educational community.

Identifying Opportunities for Leadership

The first step in building a learner leadership program is to identify high-impact areas in your school library where learner leaders can make a difference. Determine which tasks can be delegated—such as assistance at the circulation desk, shelving books, or creating displays—to free up your time for more critical areas and make a list of these potential tasks for your learner leadership team.

From our experience, it's better to start small and, as success builds, add a new task or two. It's best to start where you are comfortable; there is no right or wrong, so just go for it. You will be surprised at how quickly learners can tackle their roles and take pride in their work.

Administrative and user-service tasks are often a good place to start, and they can build valuable organizational and interpersonal skills in your learner leaders; promote skills for critical and creative thinking; and cultivate respect for and responsible use of library resources. Consider these ideas with your community:

- Process new book boxes.
  - Unpack the box and check off each book on the packing slip.
  - Stamp the inside cover with your school's "Property of" stamp.
  - Add genre-specific or other labels to each book.
- Check books in and out to other learners and faculty.
- Shelve returned books.
- Search the library management system for books.
- Create dynamic table and shelf displays for monthly events or focus.
- Maintain individual makerspace areas.
  - Create and display instructions in centers for independent use.
  - Replenish materials as needed.
  - Assist other learners with items featured in the makerspace.
  - Prepare resources for use in the makerspace.
- Create book reviews.
  - Craft recommendation cards for books.
  - Develop reading-list recommendations.
  - Write a one-pager on a book.
  - Feature QR codes for a book trailer.
  - Produce videos for an in-house news program.
- Fulfill requests for materials by educators.
- Greet visitors as they enter the school library and check for passes as needed.
- Teach users how to find materials using call numbers.
- Answer questions on navigating databases and applications.
- Assist others with citations.
- Care for special features such as fish tanks, plants, and "zen" spaces.
- Decorate library spaces with murals and signs.
- Encourage reading through personal recommendations.

Consider more challenging tasks for learner leaders, such as:

- Assist with technology hardware, including audio and smartboards.
- Cover books in protective plastic.
- Create a list to promote new books.
- Scan books when taking inventory.
- Search shelves for lost books.
- Log new magazines.

Have you come up with some new tasks that weren't mentioned here? Set your school library goals and keep the list handy for action.

Finding Your Team

Once you have your goals organized, you'll need to find your team! Determining the number of leaders you'll need to support each goal will help you to align opportunities with learners when you recruit and interview those interested and decide which learners might be a good fit.

Identify Needs and Roles

Determine how many roles and learners you need for your leadership team to support each goal or task. Consider the benefits of having captains who manage other library leaders or specific library sections—essentially creating a hierarchy within your leadership team to ensure efficient task management and scaffold leadership opportunities for learners in higher grades. Alternately, building a cohesive crew of equals also presents benefits for collaboration and teamwork.

As Dione began presenting her vision of learner leaders in the school library to her colleagues, many school librarians reached out in turn to share their success stories. In some programs, it may be better to have captains or directors who oversee other learners or specific tasks. Fellow librarian Elaine Aaron employs a learner leader approach known as "Special Ops" in her elementary school library. Each role is given a military nomenclature, such as "Sergeant at Arms" for the door greeter. Have fun selecting a theme for your library leaders' program and develop creative titles; better yet, involve your library leaders in creating the program theme.

In her school newsroom, Dione does employ a leadership hierarchy with student directors responsible for running the newsroom and managing the effectiveness of the rotating news anchors. However, in her school library leadership program, all Media TOTs are equal and share in the ownership of the school library. Every week, learners rotate jobs so that participants eventually learn all aspects of running the library successfully. Dione finds that her learner leaders work better as a cooperative unit, building in themselves and each other a strong foundation of skills as a leadership team.

WHAT'S IN A NAME?

Get creative and develop a name for your team of learner leaders (maybe use your school mascot for inspiration). Our colleagues have used the following clever monikers.

» Ambassador
» Apprentice
» Classroom Captains
» Coach
» Educator Assistant
» Library Helper
» Library Keeper
» Media Techs
» Media TOTs (Teachers of Tomorrow)
» Monitor
» School Mascot: For example, Panther or Eagle
» Special Ops
» Support

Explore what works for you, your learners, and your community. Remember, it is okay to change your mind and try a different approach the next school year and keep experimenting until you find what works best for everyone.

Gather Candidates

Many learners are naturally drawn to our school libraries, feeling at home and eager to assist. Starting with these learners can be advantageous, but there are numerous ways to approach identifying your leadership team.

- Make a general announcement on the morning news.
- Announce library leadership opportunities during your classes.
- Write an article for your school or library newsletter.
- Create a poster for display in the school library or other common areas (see sample A).

- Create an infographic and post it to social media.
- Tap learners who frequent the school library and show an interest in helping.
- Obtain recommendations from other educators.

Provide multiple avenues in your promotions for learners to express their interest in the library leadership program. Make it easy for them to respond while ensuring that your response mechanism is manageable for you and collects the information you need to determine participant opportunities. You might have learners:

- respond to an online form (see sample B, "Library Leader Interest Form"),
- write a short paragraph explaining why they would be a good fit, or
- schedule an in-person interview (see sample C, "Library Leader Interview Checklist").

Recruiting Timeline

Consider the time of year to begin selecting your team. Starting fresh at the start of each school year allows you to see which students are available and willing to participate. However, a rolling recruitment approach may better fit your school library schedule, allowing you to add new leaders throughout the year, facilitating ongoing training in situations where a new student may come into the school or a current student leader can no longer participate. Securing and training learners at the end of the school year can ensure that learners are familiar with the tasks and can shorten the refresher training when they return to school in the fall.

Screen and Select Participants

Once you've gathered a list of learners with interest in the program, a quick interview about responsibility, expectations, and procedures will follow (see sample C, "Library Leader Interview Checklist"). Assess whether they can speak comfortably to an adult. Some learners may be shy initially, but with time, they often contribute significantly. Patience is key. With timid learners, you may consider waiting until there are stronger candidates to support them. Find a comfortable approach for you.

Consulting with classroom educators can be a great way to evaluate candidates on your list for any potential behavioral concerns. Speak with educators directly or send a personal note asking if they would recommend the learner as a library leader. Their reactions can be very informative and can help build on your collaborative relationships with those educators. Checking grades can also help identify learners who might benefit most from this leadership opportunity as motivation to improve. Keep an open mind, encourage all learners to apply, and endeavor to find a suitable role for learners of all abilities.

Keep a Waitlist

Select enough learners to fill your team and then create a waitlist for the remaining candidates. Why a waitlist? Some learners leave midyear, decide to join a club or sport, or have a different schedule for the next semester, and you will need to fill those positions. Other learners will decide that this just isn't for them. Go to your waitlist to find a new leader and train them to take over that position.

Acquire Permission

Your school district may require permission slips if you operate a morning or afternoon "club" of library leaders. If you are having your leaders help with a before-school or after-school open library, or if you go on a field trip with your leadership team, utilize a permission slip that fits your needs. Your school may have a standard permission slip, but a custom version may be a better fit for running a library leadership program (see sample D, "Library Leader Parent Information Letter," and sample E, "Library Leader Permission Form").

Include pertinent information needed about the learner:

- Do they have food allergies?
- How will they get to school and/or get home from school?
- How can you contact the parent or guardian if the need arises?

Consider adding parental consent to a permission form to share pictures on communications platforms of your trainees, any special events, and daily kudos; photos like these can significantly enhance your program planning and promotion.

A behavior contract, too, instills in the learner their position's immense responsibility. Clearly state the desired behavior, allowing students and parents to understand what the expectations are for leaders, as they both sign the form. Refer back to this contract when necessary. Signing this contract is the student's first real action in accepting responsibility as a leader (see sample F, "Library Leader Behavior Contract").

Efficient communication and trust among schools, learners, and parents helps to build strong working relationships with your leaders. Examples and templates for these important foundational communications and forms are available in part II, "Forms, Templates, and Essential Tools" and also available for download at **alaeditions.org/AASLextras**—use or modify these resources to fit your needs.

Putting It into Perspective

Developing your library leadership program begins with identifying those areas that are easily delegated to create leadership opportunities. Recruiting and selecting candidates, forming relationships with your leadership teams, and obtaining necessary permissions formalizes the start of your program. Congratulate yourself on taking the initial steps in this rewarding endeavor.

3

Let's Train

Setting the stage for a successful library leadership program begins with establishing clear expectations, designing tailored sessions for training groups, and setting a flexible and adaptable training schedule to meet the needs of the leaders, the school library, and its users.

The goal is to train your library leaders to think and work independently. As your learners become proactive leaders who take initiative, their leadership skills toolbox grows. The time invested in building a strong library leadership team benefits not only the learner, but everyone involved in the school community.

Setting Clear Expectations

Learner leaders need to clearly understand their responsibilities and how to be accountable for completing each task. Equipping learners with task lists and sign-in sheets fosters a proactive mindset and sets clear expectations for achievement.

Task List

When starting the library leaders' program, create a task list with job titles and a brief description of the tasks involved to keep learners focused on their assigned duties (see sample G, "Task Descriptions for Library Leader Roles"). Consider the reading level of your participants as you describe the goals for each role and how these will be accomplished. Using simple language, be clear and concise with your descriptions to provide your trainees with a resource to refer to whenever a reminder of their duties is needed. Table 3.1 provides a few examples to get you started.

A task list allows your learners' independence and promotes initiative to familiarize themselves with the roles and tasks in the school library. Leaders review the expectations, seek peer assistance with filling knowledge gaps, and develop intrinsic pride in their job done well.[1]

Sign-In Sheet

Sign-in sheets list the jobs and roles described on your task list and designate learners who are responsible for those tasks that day or week (see sample H, "Library Leader Sign-In Sheet"). Learners check the sign-in sheet for their job each week on Monday and understand the responsibility to accomplish the related tasks every day that week. Giving the learners the same job or set of tasks for a full week builds their self-confidence and stamina. Then, as gurus of that role or task, they can easily nurture other learners who are assigned that role in subsequent weeks.

Well-developed task lists and sign-in sheets serve as a reference for learners at the start of training. Be clear about what you expect and how learners should behave while performing leadership tasks, and give praise often!

STAY ORGANIZED AND ON TRACK

Task lists and sign-in sheets:

- » help learners check their daily job,
- » remind learners of their goals and the tasks to accomplish them, and
- » provide school librarians with an attendance log.

Training Leader Groups

When developing effective training sessions, it's crucial to consider optimal group sizes and settings to maximize training and implement a scaffolded approach with hands-on experiences.[2] Hands-on training will allow participants to gain practical experience and confidence in their roles.

TABLE 3.1

Example Task Descriptions for Library Leader Roles

Job/roles	Task description
Check-in computer	Turn on the computer at the circulation desk and open our online system. Use the special circulation user name and password to log in. Click on Circulation. Be sure to select Check In and then click inside the text box before scanning the barcode of the book being returned. Remember to greet your customers, look them in the eye, and say, "Thank you!"
Door greeter	Stand at the double-door entrance and greet each school library user warmly. Remember, our doors open promptly at 7:30 a.m.
Makerspace/Lego room monitor	Open the Makerspace/Lego Room. Set out the centers you would like to have open that day. As makerspace users come in, greet them with a smile and ask if any assistance is needed. Walk around the room and offer help and encouragement. At the end of the session, remind users to help clean up their area. Put all centers back and check that the area is clean. Usher last-minute stragglers to the exit with a smile.
Shelve books: "E for Everybody" fiction carts	Wheel the "E for Everybody" trolly to the E section of the school library. Using the call number, place each book back on its correct shelf next to the other books by that same author. Remember to always use alphabetical order when placing books back on the shelf. Look for other books already on the shelf that have been mis-shelved and need to be relocated.
Shelve books: 100, 200, and 300 nonfiction	Wheel the nonfiction book trolly to the nonfiction section of the school library. Using the call number, place each book back on its correct shelf next to the other books about that same subject. Remember to always use the Dewey Decimal Classification system's numerical order when placing books back on the shelf. Look for other books already on the shelf that have been mis-shelved and need to be relocated.
Check-out computer	Turn on the computer at the circulation desk and open our online system. Use the special circulation user name and password to log in. Click on Circulation. Be sure to select Check Out and then click inside the text box and enter the library user's name before scanning the barcode of the book being selected. Remember to greet your customers, look them in the eye, and say, "Thank you!"

Optimal Group Sizes

When first developing a learner leadership program, large-group trainings at the beginning of the school year may seem efficient and effective. However, "there is a phenomenon that occurs in workplaces everywhere, known as the 80/20 rule . . . which suggests that roughly 20% of the workforce is responsible for accomplishing 80% of the work."[3] Inevitably, some of your new library leaders will be excellent in completing their tasks while others are not. Additional training throughout the year may help alleviate the problems to some extent, but not completely.

For a more effective result, break up the training into smaller groups of three or four learners per session to give more time and attention to each learner with hands-on experience in various tasks. Small groups work exceptionally well to hone skills. The goal is to:

- meet each learner at their level,
- guide them to understand the task or goal precisely,
- set expectations for completing their task,
- instill an understanding for behavior while performing the task, and
- convey the importance of each learners' role in the school library.

Through the training, your learner leaders should demonstrate their understanding of each agreed-upon task and its importance in achieving the objective. By teaching a few learners at a time and allowing them to show their mastery of a skill, your trainings will create a ripple effect: these new leaders can now take on the responsibility of training the next group. Small-group training fosters a strong working relationship with your leaders now and for the future.

Training in Action

Inspired by a desire to help all library leaders reach their potential, Dione developed a small-group training regime that has significantly benefited her elementary school library leadership program. In this model, students thrive on learning from their peers, effectively building learners' self-confidence and their proficiency in the school library while teaching them the ethical use of information, technology, and media. Learners training other learners—much like upperclassmen guiding new cadets at the Air Force Academy and the

Naval Academy—is highly effective! Through brief (30-minute) sessions before school, small groups can master tasks and train the next group of learner leaders, ensuring continuous growth and support.

Day 1: Training—Group 1

On the first day, drive home the point and importance of the organized school library with everything in the correct place, especially the books. Start this small-group training directly with you. Introduce the goals and how each task should be performed. Give time for the trainees to practice the tasks and build stamina. By practicing with you and then in learner pairs, your leaders will quickly develop the skills needed. For example, as an important foundational task, leaders can learn how to shelve returned books onto the book trollies after being checked in at the circulation desk. Labeling your book trollies clearly will help learners grasp where to put the books at the circulation desk. Have your trainees practice returning books and putting them on the appropriate carts; this makes shelving books in the stacks easier.

Once learners understand the bins, it's time to take them into the stacks and reshelve the books. Help learners understand the importance of correctly shelving books by discussing the frustration of finding a book that's listed in the catalog as available but isn't where it should be. Encourage leaders to share their own experiences with this issue. Spend time in each library area and on book placement. Praise learners' efforts and answer their questions, making them feel like an essential part of the school library team.

LIBRARY LEADERS TAKING OWNERSHIP

After Dione's first library leader training, she heard an exchange during a fourth-grade class period later that day. A new library leader remarked to another learner that a particular book had to be placed in the library—otherwise, our "library will be broken."

Day 2: Service Skills Practice—Group 1

On the second day, focus your training on customer service skills and helming the circulation desk. Teaching learners how to interact with others in a way that engenders a sense of welcoming and appreciation is no small task. Practice polite greetings and common inquiries (see figure 3.1). Small acts of kindness, such as smiling and looking directly at the person you are speaking to, bring joy to our young library customers, but this can take practice for our new library leaders.

FIGURE 3.1
School Library Greetings

BUILDING CONFIDENCE WITH ROLE-PLAYING SCENARIOS

One new library helper really struggled in helming the circulation desk—he became visibly nervous, speaking with others in a gruff manner. Quickly taking the lead, Dione modeled how to speak in a welcoming, kind way, and she practiced several scenarios with the learner. The other library leaders acted as potential customers, pretending to bring books back to the school library. After several attempts, the learner became more and more accustomed to wearing a smile and greeting others kindly. The other Media TOTs were quick with praise and helped him feel that his success was real. This activity allowed the learners to work together to create a welcoming space for each other and their customers.

Day 3: Leaders Training Leaders—Groups 1 and 2

On the third day, four new library leaders begin their training, with the trainees of group 1 helping to facilitate. Now, leaders are training leaders! Use the same two-day format focusing on the importance of library book placement by call numbers for all new trainees, now reinforced by the new trainers.

Dedicate a full training day to accurate book shelving to emphasize its importance. As group 1 oversees new trainees, guide them in providing positive feedback and corrections.[4] This process helps learners develop emotional intelligence for future collaborative work. Allow them to act as coaches and to take leadership roles. Building your library leadership team may take several weeks, and that's perfectly fine.

Day 4: Leaders Training Leaders in Service Skills Practice—Groups 1 and 2

On the fourth day, create opportunities for your leaders in both groups to practice their customer service skills while you train the next leader group on the call numbers and shelving books. For example, have leaders from group 1 act as circulation desk clerks while the new trainees from group 2 pretend to return and check out books. Have the group 1 trainers explain to the group 2 trainees why using the computer ethically is essential. Praise their small steps, such as making eye contact, smiling, greeting the "customer" in a friendly manner, asking for the customer's name and their educator's name, pointing to the screen to have the customer verify that it is their library account, scanning the book correctly, offering a free bookmark, and thanking the customer for coming into the school library. By allowing the group 1 trainers to model the tasks for group 2, you effectively make them the leaders of the training. Follow up by having circulation desk protocols practiced by the group 2 trainees, with the group 1 trainers acting as potential customers and providing feedback to the new crew.[5]

Day 5: Leaders Training Leaders—Groups 1, 2, and 3

On the fifth day, four new library leaders (group 3) will begin their training with group 2 helping to facilitate. Leaders from group 1 are now able to provide more assistance with setting up makerspace areas, creating eye-catching table displays, and organizing shelves with forward-facing books and the effective use of bookends. You'll notice that your school library is looking more organized and pleasing.

Day 6: Leaders Training Leaders in Service Skills Practice—Groups 1, 2, and 3

On the sixth day, have group 3 practice circulation desk protocols with group 2 trainers acting as potential customers and providing feedback to their new crew.[6] As you begin to see who excels with each task, those learners will become the "gurus" of that task. What does this mean? Some learners naturally gravitate to shelving books; others enjoy the customer service interactions of the circulation desk; still others prefer to set up seasonal displays. No matter the task, certain library leaders will excel in that area. Be sure to praise, praise, praise. You will need their help as you train new leaders, teaching and advising others to implement that task.

Allow all the new library leaders a moment to relish in their success. Set time aside to congratulate your team and celebrate their accomplishments—perhaps with a special "Library Leaders Only" breakfast—and get your leaders excited for opening day.

CREATING CONNECTIONS THROUGH SUCCESSFUL BOOK TRANSACTIONS

The library management system in Dione's library sometimes leads to accidental book check-outs. This means that either the book is checked out to the wrong library user, or the books are never actually checked out to anyone. Conversely, when scanning the returns, books may not scan properly and may not get taken off the patron's account. First, the learner's ID barcode must be scanned or their name entered, then the book is scanned. If the cursor is moved during this process and the field box isn't selected when a book is scanned, the online program doesn't register the book. The field or box must be in bold black outline so that the barcode scans correctly and the book is registered to the correct library user.

In the excitement of using the scanner, many learners start scanning books without regard to the actual user account or the selected field on the computer screen. To alleviate this problem, Dione sets up valuable check-in and check-out protocols; they may help at your library, too.

1. When a library user comes up to the circulation desk to check out a book, the library leader either scans the user's ID or types in the name.
2. The library leader points to the user's name on the computer screen and has the user verify it. It's like saying, "Yes, that's me!"
3. The library leader scans the book's barcode to the correct account. Ensuring that the field box is selected and appears in bold outline helps the library leader know that the information has been entered correctly.
4. The library user can then confirm that their book is entered properly in their account. When scanning a returned book, the library leader points to the screen to show the user that the book has been properly returned.

But it's not just about books; it's about connecting with library users. When library leaders smile and thank learners and educators for visiting, they build goodwill and create a warm, inviting atmosphere in the school library. So, when you witness this happening, be thrilled! Let your leaders know they're doing an excellent job—it's like giving them a gold star for their library service.

BOOSTING SELF-ESTEEM AND CREATING IDENTITY

End each training day with a moment to come together, praise each other, and talk about how to make the program even better. One bright young leader in Dione's program asked if name tags could be used so that their customers would know who to ask for help. We quickly decided to use our button maker to make Media TOT name tags. Now everyone knows the Media TOTs, and the new leaders are so proud to wear their buttons.

Another idea that Diana's library leaders use is to create a sign that lists the names of the leaders on that shift, displayed in a plexiglass holder at the circulation desk. This simple act allows library users to know who is assisting them and encourages interactions between the library users and leaders.

When to Train

Just as important as *how* you train is *when* you train your library leaders. There are benefits to each approach, whether you train at the start of the year, at the end of the year, or employ a rolling start. Consider your needs thoughtfully, along with the needs of your school library and your community of learners to determine when would be the best time for your library leadership program training.

Start of the Year

Diana has had the most success working with the school library clerk and several knowledgeable learners to conduct learner leadership training during one high school class period (55 to 90 minutes) at the beginning of the school year. Together, they plan an agenda and an outline for the training. It begins with an orientation, followed by thorough training on each machine.

When library leader trainings are on her class roster, the "Library Leader Skills Checklist" (sample I) serves as a guide and rubric for what leaders need to know to assist themselves and the school library users. It allows the training educator to assess each library leader's performance and quickly provide them with a grade for the class.

Library leader training starts on the second day of class with teacher assistants (TAs). Seniors are trained in groups of five to twenty-five, depending on their period assignment. This approach enables Diana's high school leaders to start helping quickly. Leaders are encouraged to help each other, solve problems independently, and report issues. Once a few learner leaders are trained, they in turn offer training to new leaders with support from other TAs or media techs.

ONBOARDING TALKING POINTS

Focus your initial training session onboarding or orientation for library leaders. There will be other opportunities for training as learners show increased capability and interest in more-complex tasks. It is impossible to cover everything in a single training session, so limit your lecture/talking points to the most important aspects for learners "working" in the school library and representing their educators:

- signing in for duty
- professionalism
- greeting library users
- conduct
- expectations
- attire
- alerting library staff to problems, such as machines that do not work

End of the Year

The beginning of the school year seemed to be a good fit for training when Dione first started the leadership program in her elementary school library; learners were selected and trained in the first month of school. However, the next year, Dione basically started from scratch, all over again.

Identifying potential candidates for the next year's fourth-grade Media TOTs from the present year's third-grade classes allows prospective leaders to shine. During the final month of school, learners request to become Media TOTs. After Dione gathers names of learners interested in becoming Media TOTs, she shares the list with classroom educators to ask for their reflective feedback on the leadership qualities and potential of each learner. Then she creates the list of next year's Media TOTs. Using the current team to train new leaders fosters a dynamic and inclusive program. Fourth-graders proudly perform tasks alongside third-graders, who admire their skills. By the start of the new school year, Media TOTs are ready to welcome peers into the school library from the first week.

This advance training reduces the need for start-of-school training, allowing the school library to open quickly and provide a welcoming, safe space for all learners to think, create, share, and grow.

Rolling Start

When new learners are placed in leadership roles throughout the school year, rolling training must be deployed. Introduce them to the school library team, including the learner leaders who have already been trained and are working throughout library areas. During the tour, new leaders receive on-the-spot training from the library leaders working in each area, from educators at the station or machine, and from the library clerk or the school librarian.

The Library Leaders TASK (To Assist and Share Knowledge) List can be compared to the outcome of a weekly meeting between the school librarian and the library clerk, which is a successful routine utilized at Diana's school. They aim to meet each Monday. In these weekly meetings, they discuss each week's goals and the best strategies for accomplishing them, and then they create a list of tasks to implement their plan. The resulting TASK list helps Diana and the library clerk stay focused on their goals and allows library leaders to see where they can assist. The example in figure 3.2 is of a random week; some weeks feature more entries than others.

Recording your training material can be a useful tool to facilitate rolling starts and guarantee that school library procedures are maintained, supporting an orderly and reliable system. Direct new leaders to how-to videos on various tasks that can be watched as needed. Trained learners returning at the start of the school year can provide help in the library even before the first training for new library leaders begins. Recorded material can serve as a helpful refresher after summer break or for returning leaders who are performing an unfamiliar task.

FIGURE 3.2
Example Weekly TASK List for Library Leaders

Media Tech TASK List

(**T**o **A**ssist and **S**hare **K**nowledge)
To accomplish this week of 1/27–31/2025

1. We are celebrating Literacy Week in Florida. Be ready to share a favorite book with a library user. How many students can you get to check out books?
2. Get ready for Kerry O'Malley Cerra's author visit Tuesday—PLEASE BE ON YOUR BEST BEHAVIOR. Welcome guests and get students seated so the author can begin 10 minutes into each period (periods 1 and 3–6).
3. Check Canvas and FOCUS for your grades and assignments.
4. Move tables and create audience seating with chairs. Make an aisle in the center—do not block exits or books.
5. Check the to-do list at the circulation desk and with Mrs. Anders and Mrs. Haneski regarding deliveries and jobs to do.
6. Media Techs: Have an iPad ready to use the library management system to search for available books on our shelves.
7. Information on Book/Makerspace/Mind-Body Clubs available at the circulation desk.
8. Are you reading a book for pleasure? Look for a book you want to read and read it.
9. Get familiar with the apps and features of Microsoft 365 and use them.
10. Locate Florida Teens Read (FTR) books and information.
11. Link to reliable, accurate, and up-to-date resources starting at our school website.
12. Look around and help where needed today.

Thank you. Your efforts and help are appreciated.
—Mrs. Haneski

When Diana's colleague, the high school library clerk, was scheduled for surgery and unable to attend the first week of school, the library leaders' program developed valuable resources to fill any gaps in library service and training. For example, leaders were asked to film training for various workroom machines; this content was uploaded to Canvas, serving as a refresher for new-leader arrivals and as a resource for library users and parents.

Once trained, library leaders were tasked with using paper cutters to trim and laminate their printed ID badges. Observing them learn from and assist each other was rewarding. Those who finished early proudly helped others, fostering a collaborative environment.

Learners are encouraged to be well rounded and to master all tasks. In this case, learners could showcase their specialties by developing recorded training for others on various library aspects, building their self-esteem, pride, and ownership in the school library.

Putting It into Perspective

To effectively train library leaders, clearly define their roles, adopt a flexible training approach that accommodates different schedules, and focus on meeting each learner at their current skill level. This allows for customized training programs that cater to individual needs and foster wide-ranging growth. Our aim is for learners to develop independent thinking and working skills. Encourage them to use their common sense, to reflect on their learning and actions, to ask questions, and to respect others, the school library resources, and themselves.

After all the training is completed and you are confident in your leadership team, it's time for your library leaders to shine! Open the doors and let your library users enter your new learner-empowered school library. Walk around, notice accomplishments, and praise your leaders as they work toward their goals. Give sincere praise to each leader as you witness their success. Gently guide anyone who needs a little extra help. You are building relationships. And yes, give yourself a big high-five—you made this possible!

PASSIVE POSITIVITY

Everybody needs a little boost sometimes. Create a bulletin board filled with positive messages written on sticky notes that learners can take whenever they need encouragement. Alternatively, place the notes in a "Box of Love," allowing learners to pull out a special positive message to brighten their day. Placing strategic quotes around the school library helps everyone. It's a simple and passive way to encourage your learners and library leaders. Some of our favorites are:

Never give up, for that is just the place and time that the tide will turn.—*Harriet Beecher Stowe, Oldtown Folks, 1869*

Tell me and I forget. Teach me and I remember. Involve me and I learn.—*Xunzi, Xun Kuang, 818 AD*

NOTES

1. AASL American Association of School Librarians, *National School Library Standards for Learners, School Librarians, and School Libraries*, 2nd ed. (American Library Association, 2026), Learner I.A.1.: "Learners display curiosity and initiative by formulating questions," and Learner III.B.2.: "Establishing connections with other learners to build on their own prior knowledge and create new knowledge."
2. AASL, *National School Library Standards*, School Librarian V.D.1.: "Scaffolding iterative challenge-response processes."
3. Personnel Perspective, "The 80/20 rule: Understanding Why 20% of the Workforce Does 80% of the Work," January 19, 2024, personnelperspective.com/2024/01/19/the-80-20-rule-understanding-why-20-of-the-workforce-does-80-of-the-work.
4. AASL, *National School Library Standards*, School Librarian III.C.1.: "Demonstrating how to solicit and respond to feedback from others."
5. AASL, *National School Library Standards*, School Librarian III.A.2.: "Scaffolding enactment of learning-group roles to enable the development of new understandings within a group."
6. AASL, *National School Library Standards*, Learner I.C.2.: "Providing constructive feedback," and Learner III.C.1.: "Soliciting and responding to feedback from others."

4

Unlocking Leadership Potential

Developing future leaders in school libraries relies on the effectiveness of the school librarian. Just as keys unlock doors, the school librarian can use certain keys to unlock the leadership potential of their learners. By modeling a multifaceted approach to best practices reinforced through specific praise and feedback, school librarians can guide learners' interactions with others by encouraging problem-solving, ensuring accountability, and promoting self-reflection, thereby unlocking learners' leadership potential.

Modeling Leadership and Positive Reinforcement

The nature of our position comes with many opportunities to model best practices. Modeling key leadership practices gives your learners a set of leadership tools and helps build their confidence, nurture self-efficacy, foster intrinsic motivation, and ignite the desire to excel. When school librarians turn these keys, learners are empowered to navigate their own path, adjusting their approach as needed, and fill their toolbox with leadership skills. School librarians are able to reinforce leadership models and skill sets by offering praise (figure 4.1) and demonstrating effective feedback for positive growth.[1]

Library leaders and volunteers want to be helpful, have a purpose, and feel appreciated. It is a mood booster to observe them skipping to the shelves for a book or gleefully opening a new box of books and squealing with delight. Put the time in to train these young leaders—they will be an asset to your program for years.

It's essential to demonstrate constructive feedback to guide and build the leadership skill set needed so that the action is worthy of the praise. Specific

FIGURE 4.1
How to Give Praise

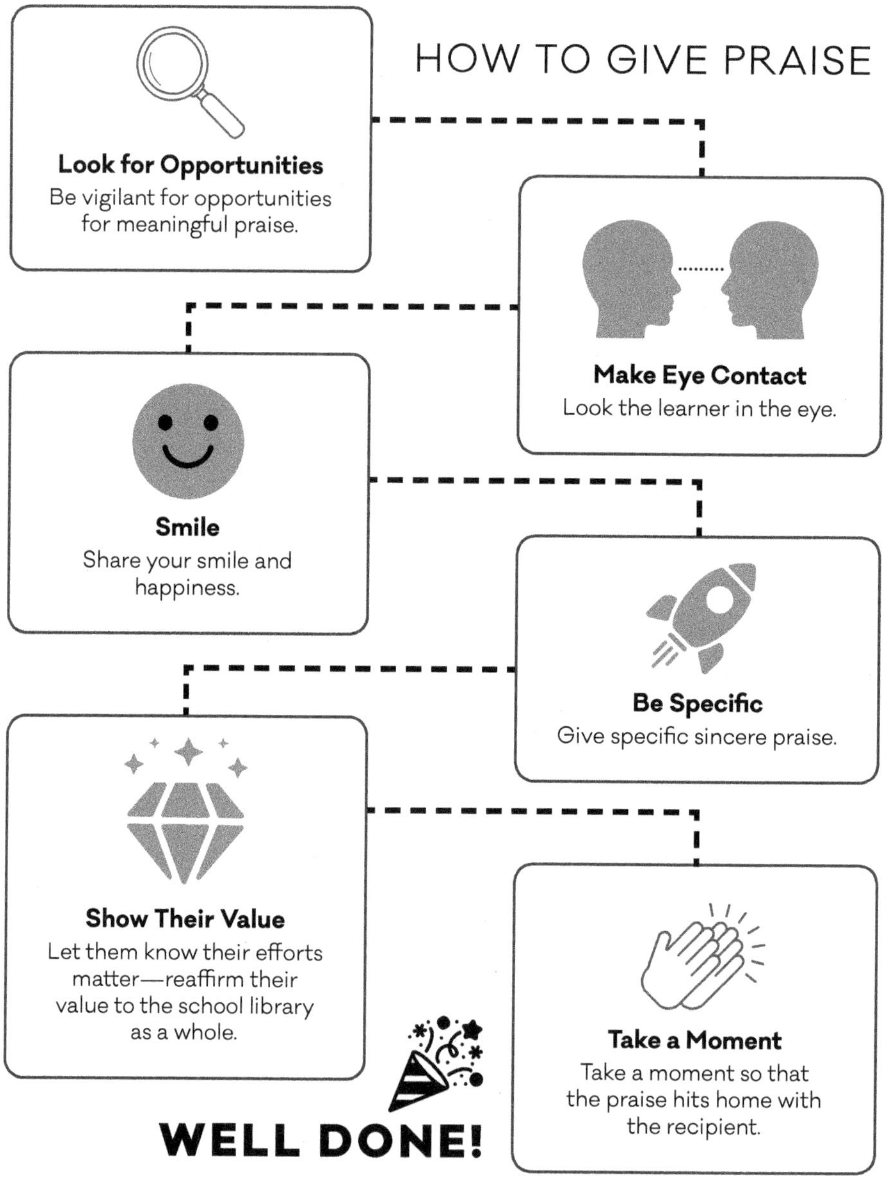

praise motivates the learner and those listening around them. Show enthusiasm when library leaders arrive for training. Thank them for their time working to help the school library, and express excitement for the benefits they gain from the experience. The smiles on their faces show their confidence to give the school library 100% effort and to be essential helpers and team members.

Managing Interruptions Respectfully

It's important to train library leaders in a real-world setting to show how to handle hectic times. When learners observe specifically how you navigate interruptions, it allows them to understand how to manage their own time without disrupting learning, as well as how to provide good customer service and respond to others kindly as a library leader. Teaching learners how to respond to others with poise is a valuable tool for their personal growth and success when they are adjusting their awareness, demonstrating empathy, and interacting with others who may reflect a range of perspectives.[2]

During a training session for Diana's high school library leaders, she needed to interrupt the library clerk, who was leading the training. Knowing her leaders were observing, she said politely, "Excuse me," and waited for acknowledgment before she asked a brief question. Concluding the interaction with "Pardon the interruption and thank you" also demonstrated to the trainees the proper way to handle interruptions.

In a school library open throughout the day, learners will observe your behavior. Other educators may interrupt while you're working with learners. Depending on the request, it's okay to say, "I wish I could help at this time, but I can't right now." Model this for your library leaders. Show interest in the educator's need but kindly let them know you'll handle it after you finish, after school, or another time. Suggest that the educator email their request for easier or faster resolution.

HANDLING INTERRUPTIONS LIKE A PRO

Teach learner volunteers how to answer the phone correctly and professionally.

- » Answer the phone with "Media Center, [*learner's name or student*] speaking—how may I help you?"
- » Listen to the phone request.
- » If the caller hasn't given their name yet, say: "May I ask who is calling?"
- » Next, say: "Thank you—let me check if the person you need is available at the moment."
- » Engage the person requested if that person is available. If not, take a message [*next step*].
- » Say: "I'm sorry, but that person is not available at this moment. May I take a message and have your call returned?"
- » Take the message. Keep paper and pencils by the phone for this purpose.
- » End the call with: "Thank you for calling. Happy reading!"

This process takes a few seconds to explain but gives your library leaders valuable skills in presenting themselves when answering the phone and taking detailed messages. Be nearby for support and to observe. Give a quick assessment of their approach. Did the learner get it right? Give the appropriate praise and feedback, and let them self-reflect—the learner will be ready to answer the phone for you with renewed motivation.

Library leaders can often become distracted themselves once the school library opens and their friends come pouring in. When shelving books, learners often engage with classmates. By gently guiding them back to their work and teaching them how to handle distractions, you allow the learner to grow in performing a task and give them strategies to deal with people and interruptions in their own lives. Encourage your leaders to stay focused and strive for success. Try to spot them interacting with their peers while using the customer service skills you have taught, and give praise so your leaders know when they have done something right.

Encouraging Problem-Solving

Problem-solving initiative is a key component to training learners as future leaders in the school library and beyond. A valuable key teaching strategy is "Ask Three before Me," where learners try three ways to figure out the problem among themselves. If unsuccessful, the learners then ask the educator. Implement this strategy when working with all library leaders. Why? Strive to build a community of learners who can communicate and share ideas in the school library. Pairing an experienced leader with a new trainee can encourage communication and problem-solving, developing confidence, collaboration, and creative thinking skills for both leaders. By teaching learners that the tools needed to solve problems are within their grasp, you set them up for success not only as library leaders but as valuable members of society.

Applaud learners that try to solve a problem and succeed. Even if they're unsuccessful at their first attempt, encourage them to keep trying by giving subtle hints to help them find a solution. Share with them the motto "If at first you don't succeed, try, try, again." As learners begin to trust their capabilities, you will find their individual growth to be exponential.

When mistakes or accidents happen, school librarians can model problem-solving behavior, reducing a learner's stress and fear of errors. Show your leaders that mistakes are learning opportunities by focusing on solutions instead of displaying agitation. Be open when you, yourself, make a mistake. Talk about the problem and the potential solutions out loud so learners can see your calm reactions and gratitude for learning.

PROBLEM-SOLVING IN ACTION

One day in Diana's high school library, a library leader placed a full box of copy paper on a table, causing a caster to break off. The learner informed Diana of the issue, and together with another leader moved the broken table to the back room to prevent injuries. The school library staff assembled to problem-solve the situation. The clerk discovered that the broken caster could be removed, prompting the library leaders to remove the remaining casters. The group brainstormed solutions to salvage the table and avoid scratching the floor. The solution: strong black tape and cardboard padding. The table was quickly fixed and put back in place during the same class period. By allowing her leaders to engage in problem-solving, Diana encouraged and supported their ability to work collaboratively in a real-world situation.

Being open to showing our mistakes and modeling our process to create solutions helps leaders in training see how easy it is to learn from mistakes and build problem-solving skills. This modeling and encouragement also helps build your relationships with learners as they begin to value the partnership of school library staff and their leader peers working as a team to support the school library—a critical factor in their leadership development.[3] Opportunities where learners can communicate, collaborate, and learn from peers when solving problems are vital in building strong leaders for tomorrow and great library leaders today!

Ensuring Accountability

When a leader isn't fulfilling their task, take the time to retrain them, either in small groups or one-on-one. Show them you believe in their potential. For some learners, this may be their first significant responsibility, as they might not have had household chores or jobs in high school. Help your leaders understand the importance of accountability and doing a job well.

It's perfectly fine to give quick direct instructions and observe the outcome. If issues arise, address them swiftly without fuss. For example, "Couldn't find that book? Let's have another set of eyes help locate it." Or, "This paper needs to be cut straight to fit in the holder—let me [or another experienced leader] show you how to use the ruler and edge on the paper cutter for practice."

Remember that there will be times when a new leader tests the boundaries of your library leadership program. You may have a learner who just wants to play instead of completing the tasks assigned each week. Their behavior creates animosity among the other leaders and undermines all you've accomplished to get the library leadership program working. It's time to take that learner and give valuable one-on-one redirection and training. Look for the area that seems to be a success for them.

In one such instance, a leader in Dione's TOTs program decided that hanging out with friends was more fun than doing his task in the school library. First, Dione asked the learner if he understood the task that was expected of him.[4] Upon confirming that shelving books was boring and he just didn't want to do it, she redirected his views to a more positive outlook. It was imperative that he find his niche,[5] so she spent time shelving nonfiction books with him. It took a lot of patience and guidance to train this learner to understand shelving by Dewey numbers. After three days of one-on-one training, he began to understand and succeed in shelving the books. Dione gave the learner sincere praise and told him how valuable he was to the school library, letting that sink in while maintaining eye contact and a huge smile. His face beamed with pride, and he became their nonfiction guru. He then took it upon himself to train others struggling with shelving nonfiction.[6] His friends, who were a previous distraction, marveled at his knowledge of the nonfiction section and often asked him for the location of a favorite sports or animal book. He performed better in math, too, having worked with the Dewey Decimal Classification system! Dione even observed him giving sincere praise to his fellow leaders. That is where the satisfaction for school librarians lies in a learner leadership program—when scaffolded opportunities to practice inquiry build a learner's competency and confidence, and seemingly overnight you watch them blossom into lifelong learners and leaders.

Promoting Self-Reflection

One essential but often overlooked key to leadership growth is self-reflection. As the library leaders receive training and begin to focus on their work, allow some time at regular intervals for them to reflect on their successes and opportunities or areas for growth.[7] Discuss what is going well and where additional guidance is needed. Ask your leaders which tasks they feel they have mastered sufficiently, and why. In the beginning, many learners need more time to become comfortable speaking up. Teaching your library leaders to evaluate their own performance, as well as to feel confident speaking up to offer suggestions, helps the learners build a strong, self-empowered character. By stimulating learners to actively contribute and by creating a supportive environment, school librarians empower learners to see and initiate learning as a social responsibility.[8]

Diana likes to have chats while the leaders enjoy a treat of hot chocolate or tea. Giving time to her leaders provides an opportunity to communicate in a calm supportive environment. A simple "How is it going?" will elicit a response such as "I love putting the books in order on the book trolly," or "It's hard to help someone find a book."

Encourage discussion about failure and success. Having a reflective rubric (see sample J, "Library Leader Reflection Rubric") to guide conversation helps both the learner and the school librarian. Which tasks require more practice? Ask for ideas or feedback on how to improve the training or leader roles and tasks. It can also be beneficial to let leaders have a few minutes of quiet time in the school library at the end of their daily work period to reflect, write, read, or just collect themselves and be ready for their next class. When school librarians and other educators openly discuss their own mistakes and approach challenges with a positive, growth-oriented mindset, it demonstrates for learners that errors are a natural part of learning and growth. Being open about your own self-reflection process helps learners understand that everyone makes mistakes sometimes and that making mistakes is perfectly okay. You may have some learners who are perfectionists and are afraid to make mistakes. Give praise to library leaders who ask for additional instruction.

Self-reflection is a critical piece in the training of library leaders and an area where the AASL Standards are modeled through learners and the school librarian. Keep it brief—it's just a quick check-in—but let your library leaders know that their actions and ideas matter.

Putting It into Perspective

Unlocking leadership potential in our learners involves a multifaceted approach that relies on the school librarian's ability to demonstrate respectful conduct, encourage problem-solving, ensure accountability, and promote self-reflection. By modeling these key leadership practices and reinforcing behaviors through praise and feedback, school librarians will nurture strong relationships with their library leaders. Give yourself the time to focus on these steps to develop learners' confidence, skills, and self-worth. Now, take a moment to watch your super leaders shine and know you were the golden key to their success.

NOTES

1. AASL American Association of School Librarians, *National School Library Standards for Learners, School Librarians, and School Libraries*, 2nd ed. (American Library Association, 2026), School Librarian V.D.3.: "Fostering an atmosphere in which constructive feedback is openly accepted for positive growth."
2. AASL, *National School Library Standards*, School Librarian II.B.1.: "Providing opportunities for learners to interact with others who reflect a range of perspectives."
3. AASL, *National School Library Standards*, School Librarian III.B.2.: "Cultivating networks that allow learners to build on their own prior knowledge and create new knowledge."
4. AASL, *National School Library Standards*, School Librarian I.A.2.: "Activating learners' prior and background knowledge as context for constructing new meaning."
5. AASL, *National School Library Standards*, School Librarian I.D.2.: "Constructing tasks focused on learners' individual areas of interest."
6. AASL, *National School Library Standards*, Learner III.D.2.: "Recognizing learning is a social responsibility."
7. AASL, *National School Library Standards*, School Librarian V.D.2.: "Helping learners to recognize capabilities and skills that can be developed, improved, and expanded."
8. AASL, *National School Library Standards*, School Librarian III.D.1.: "Stimulating learners to actively contribute to group discussions," and School Librarian III.D.2.: "Creating a learning environment in which learners understand that learning is a social responsibility."

5

Positive Redirection

In our journey of guiding library leaders, we encounter moments when providing constructive criticism or feedback on errors becomes essential. While redirection can be intricate, learners may understandably wish to avoid hearing about their shortcomings. However, when a learner possesses all the necessary skills but fails to execute a task as requested or makes critical mistakes, it's an opportune time for positive redirection. This approach helps learners gain insights into what they need to do differently. Turning to *The New One Minute Manager* by Ken Blanchard and Spencer Johnson gives us a road map for effective redirection.

Steps to Redirection

Employing redirection will earn learners' appreciation for your empathy and build a strong working relationship. This step-by-step approach is a convenient and effective way to handle learner behavior and help library leaders reach their potential.

Step 1: Make close contact.

First, make brief or close contact when you see a mistake. This immediate action is crucial, as it addresses the issue before it escalates. Look the learner straight in the eye. This simple act gets the learner's attention and stops the behavior from continuing. Looking the learner in the eye also lets them know they are essential to you.

Step 2: Review expectations.

In 30 seconds or less, calmly go over the task or goal. Does the learner understand what they need to accomplish? This is critical—the learner may not fully understand or remember what the task expectations are. Give yourself the opportunity to empathize and meet the learner where they are.

Clarify the goal. If the learner truly has a misunderstanding of the task assigned to them, take ownership of the issue and clarify the goal. Review the task list and practice with your learner. You may also choose to have another library leader shadow that learner while they relearn the task.

Continue with the redirection. If the learner does understand what is expected, continue with the redirection. Remember that this is a valuable learning experience for your trainee and yourself.

Step 3: Be specific.

Be specific in the task that has gone off track. Avoid piling on any other issues or misdeeds. Focus on only that specific task and this specific instance.

Step 4: Verbalize your feelings.

Share your feelings about the mistake itself. Are you annoyed, angry, frustrated? Be specific about what the learner did and how it made you feel. Address the behavior only—not the person.

Step 5: Allow a moment of silence.

After expressing your feelings, allow for a moment of silence. This step is highly effective, as it lets learners think about their behavior and its impact on themselves and the school library. Giving the learner time to contemplate their actions in a supportive environment builds their self-worth and allows the learner to internalize their responsibility.

Step 6: Reinforce the expectation.

Restate the task expectations clearly. Most importantly, make it clear that this error should not be repeated.

Step 7: Express your confidence in the learner's abilities.

Again, looking the learner in the eye, tell them you believe in their competency. This step reaffirms the learner's belief in their value to you and takes the sting out of the redirection, making them feel valued and capable.

Step 8: Let it go.

Once it's over, *drop it!* Do not harbor ill will or keep bringing up the mistake over and over. No one wants to be reminded of their errors. When you drop the issue, you tell the learner that you genuinely believe they can do better.[1] A valuable lesson for any maturing individual is the belief that we all make mistakes but deserve the grace of forgiveness to do better.

Redirection In Action

Will you get this right the first time you try it? Maybe, or you may need a couple of tries. That is okay. Let your learners know when you make mistakes, and apologize. By taking ownership of your flaws, you are teaching your learners that we all make mistakes and that we grow in how we accept and deal with our own failings.[2] The point is that you are trying, and soon you will become a master at redirection.

Working with Leadership

One year, Dione had a well-trained and capable learner serving as director for the elementary news show. However, this learner needed to further develop her people skills. When it was time to bring on the new anchors for their two-week stint on the news, this director was screaming at the other learners. Rushing to her side, Dione calmly redirected her away from the group and quietly asked her to explain. The director pointed out that the new anchors weren't following her directions, and she was trying to get them to listen and do what she wanted. Understanding this is a learned behavior, Dione realized that giving this young learner a new set of tools for dealing with life's frustrations was imperative.

Looking the director in the eye, Dione calmly told her that screaming at people wasn't acceptable. Dione told her how disappointed she was when she heard screaming in the newsroom and how sad she felt for the new anchors who didn't know their jobs yet. Describing the situation from the viewpoint of others—in this case, the new anchors—presented an opportunity to instill empathy in this learner. Then, looking the learner straight in the eye, Dione fell silent.

Was the learner uncomfortable? Yes! But it drove home the point. Then, Dione expressed her belief in the director's ability to communicate in a calm, mature way that would ensure that the new anchors met her commands. Taking a moment, they brainstormed some positive ways to gain people's attention. Dione praised the director's abilities and value to the news program. Then she told the director that this same mistake of yelling would not be welcome again. And that was it! Dione never brought it up again. During the daily end of broadcast self-evaluation, the director did ask Dione for some additional ways to get the attention of her crew without resorting to screaming.[3] Some ideas were discussed, and Dione reinforced her belief in the director's abilities. That was it! Nothing more, nothing less. Giving these learners the tools to handle life's obstacles doesn't take much time, but it is invaluable in the life of that young learner.

Maya Angelou said, "I've learned that people will forget what you said, people will forget what you did, but people will never forget how you made them feel."[4] Allow these words of wisdom to guide your practice with learners. As you engage with library leaders and learners, remain mindful that an excess of criticism can deflate their enthusiasm. Instead, aim for your words to serve as a positive driving force. Remember, encouragement and constructive feedback can be powerful motivators.

Preparing Leaders to Work with Library Users

When library leaders are training in the importance of customer service with school library visitors, they learn that users come to the school library for many reasons. Sometimes, it takes a while to understand what those motives are. It's tricky and mostly a new concept for our young leaders. An enthusiastic library leader will sometimes be a bit curt or too assertive.

Remind your leaders and yourself to take a breath, to consider that people can have a bad day, and to learn from their mistakes. Most people, no matter our age, don't want to be reprimanded or called out for our mistakes, but we know it's part of growing and being the best version of ourselves. Take a moment to remind yourself to say the minimum with the most impact for action. Before you address the issue, wait to observe and show in your expression that you have something to say and need to talk. Other school library users do not need to hear what you are about to convey to the visiting learners and library leaders who are starting to disrupt the peace. Walk to a quiet area in the school library with the library user and library leader to illustrate better choices and appropriate behavior. Provide an example of another choice of words in response to the learner trying to come in for help and not being successful in clearly expressing their needs.

FROM BOSSY TO BRILLIANT

One learner was an eager yet abrasive high school library leader. Diana needed to suggest alternative responses and redirect the learner's social behaviors. Often interrupting conversations, mumbling at a rapid pace, and struggling with social interactions, this learner needed a positive role model. Diana knew it was worth the time investment.

Being mindful of setting expectations for this individual to help her grow in her interpersonal communication skills, the school library staff worked to support her needs. Modeling how to answer the phone, offering suggestions with appropriate phrases, and allowing her opportunities to practice these skills helped develop the relational skills this learner desperately needed.

One day, noticing this leader's gruff and stern demeanor toward library users, Diana gently led her away from the circulation desk to speak privately. Asking her to use kind words and to listen to the other learners' needs, Diana modeled how to interact with school library users. Catching this student leader doing the right thing and offering praise also reinforced her value to the school library and the library leadership program. The leader's questions and suggestions showed how much she cared about the school library. Often offering additional assistance—such as creating signage and helping patrons—while maintaining curiosity about school library operations, this individual developed the leadership qualities that would sustain her in her future endeavors.

She recently graduated and became a good assistant and friend at the school library. Diana couldn't be more proud of her.

Being Consistent

Consistency is essential in redirection. All library leaders must follow the same set of rules. Allowing one person or group of people to bend the rules without consequences undermines the entire library leadership program.

Even top leaders may overlook school library rules, requiring redirection. Address the situation with the tools provided here calmly, swiftly, and effectively, and the other library leaders will learn that the rules apply to everyone. The library leadership program is about building an effective, cohesive unit.

Keeping a vigilant eye on the dynamics of the school library allows the librarian to weather any storm that may arise. Use effective tools consistently to navigate your library leadership program to success.

Learning from Our Learners

As we empower learners to take on leadership roles in the school library and oversee their own growth, a delightful moment arises when we gain insights from our learners.

Educators gain insight during lessons and activities when they are open to learning from their apprentices. Watching others succeed and fail, soak in a concept before attempting it themselves, search multiple resources, and try something new when they are ready (and sometimes even before) provides school librarians and other educators an opportunity to gain confidence in our own abilities as well. This lesson in growth empowers your learners and librarians alike.

Observe learners tackling tasks in unique ways that are distinct from your own approach. Share with the library leaders that learning from their innovative methods is a joyous day for you. Be proud to be the guide on the side rather than the sage on the stage.

Putting It into Perspective

People dislike destructive criticism, and our learners are no exception. Keeping a calm, consistent, and effective set of tools for positive redirection in your pocket will build the leadership team you want and deserve. Just like a guidebook can show you the way on a road trip, these tools for positive redirection can serve you on your journey with your library leaders. Practice and use them when the need arises. Our library leaders must know they will receive our training, support, and guidance as needed. Above all, they have our respect and gratitude.

NOTES

1. AASL American Association of School Librarians, *National School Library Standards for Learners, School Librarians, and School Libraries*, 2nd ed. (American Library Association, 2026), School Librarian V.D.2.: "Helping learners to recognize capabilities and skills that can be developed, improved, and expanded."
2. AASL, *National School Library Standards*, School Librarian V.D.3.: "Fostering an atmosphere in which constructive feedback is openly accepted for positive growth."
3. AASL, *National School Library Standards*, School Librarian V.A.2.: "Challenging learners to reflect and question assumptions and possible misconceptions."
4. Maya Angelou, *I Know Why the Caged Bird Sings* (Random House, 1969), 93.

6

Cultivating Success

Introducing a library leadership program will create the dynamic school library that you have hoped for, dreamed of, and planned. An effective library leadership program will enhance your abilities to provide service, add to your learners' leadership toolbox, and solidify the belief that you can build a strong team of learner leaders in your school library.

Create Checkpoints

Checkpoints serve as a foundation for assessing and evaluating your library leadership program's progress, ensuring it's on track, and implementing necessary corrective measures (figure 6.1). They also allow you to see ahead to where you want to take your leadership program. Decide when you will set these phases: quarterly, semesterly, or another time frame that works for you.

Review Your Original Goals

Pull out your original goal or task list. Are your library leaders able to accomplish all you had hoped? Look at the supports you put in place for your learners. Are the task descriptions and sign-in sheets easy to comprehend and follow? Have you discovered that your leadership team is thriving? If your program is meeting your expectations, give yourself a huge high five!

FIGURE 6.1

Checkpoints for School Library Leaders' Success

CHECKPOINTS FOR SUCCESS

1 **Review your original goals.**
Are the leaders meeting expectations?

2 **Review challenges.**
Have you discovered roadblocks?
- Modify expectations.
- Build new expectations.

3 **Look for new growth.**
Employ new opportunities for leaders to take ownership.

4 **CELEBRATE YOUR SUCCESS!**

Review Challenges or Roadblocks

Have you uncovered an unforeseen roadblock to your program? How will you deal with this temporary setback? Assess and determine a course of action for dealing with obstacles in the school library. Will you need to modify your expectations, or will you need to build new expectations? The choice is up to you. Remember that you are your learners' mentor and that their success highly revolves around your support and guidance.

Modify Your Expectations

Decide if the roadblock requires a change or modification of your expectations. How can this obstacle be overcome? Remember when Dione shared her frustrations with some of her library leaders not performing their tasks? That was a pivotal moment. She took a hard look at her training methods and realized she could improve. Deciding to start the training during the last month of school allowed her current leaders to assist in the training of new leaders, training with much smaller groups made for a more effective training process. Roadblocks to your success are not uncommon, but it is how you deal with them that will make or break your library leadership program. Have faith in your own ability to overcome these obstacles and build a stronger program.

Build New Expectations

Does the task you originally created need to be changed—either adjusted slightly, or perhaps overhauled completely? Are there any responsibilities that are beyond the abilities of your leaders? If so, take a moment to think about what it is that you would like to see happen and how that might be better broken down into smaller tasks that are more easily accomplished by your library leaders.

Originally, Diana had tasked her leaders with laminating items for other educators and herself. But sometimes, the aging machine would jam up from static cling, rolling back the laminated items. Unjamming the machine was difficult and time consuming. Realizing this obstacle needed a new approach, Diana brainstormed a better way for her leaders to help with this task. The older machine worked well when used by only a few trained, experienced people. Diana decided to task only her experienced library leaders with lamination jobs to have ready the next day for pickup or delivery.

Diana applied this same strategy to her copy machines as well. Copiers now show step-by-step instructions on clearing a jam, and in most cases, if these guides are used, the machine will work. By building a new expectation for the tasks, Diana provided opportunities for learners' growth.

Identify Opportunities for Future Growth

While a school librarian watches library leaders flourish, future projects will inevitably take hold in their mind. Review your original tasks and goals for new opportunities for assistance from learners. Highlight innovative opportunities for your library leaders to take ownership of tasks and assist you in building a stronger school library.

Practical Applications

Reflect on the potential benefits of the library leadership program for your learners, yourself, and the school library, and allow these success stories to serve as your inspiration.

Classroom Visits Promoting Books

Promotion of the state book lists encourages visitors to look at the choices and check out a book. Circulation also improves when learners hear their peers say a book is worth reading, so Diana's library leaders visit classrooms to deliver short booktalks—an English language arts class, a study hall, or any class where an educator requests a visit. A classroom booktalk program is quick and straightforward to get started. Consider giving the learners a choice of the books they want to promote—this encourages a more passionate booktalk. Ideally, library leaders will have read the book. In this particular case, the state book list comes with annotations and descriptions of the story and genre for 15 books, so the leaders are also able to talk about the books based on the information provided. When the learners from these classrooms visit the school library, they will find book displays created by the library leader who delivered the booktalk in the classroom or on the learner-led morning news program. Get the school community involved by promoting opportunities to share their own book reviews and recommendations. Provide learners with a "Recommended Reads Form" (Sample K) near the circulation desk to fill out. Library leaders can share the forms received by reading them on the morning news program. As forms are received, learners are invited to appear on the morning news to deliver their own booktalk. If the learner is uncomfortable about appearing live on the news program, then a library leader may read it for them. Some learners may not want their recommendation broadcast to the whole school, so allow them to place their written review inside the front cover of the book or in a plexiglass sign holder on the bookshelf next to the book, creating a "Recommended Reads" feature within your library. By participating in this library initiative and giving booktalks to promote reading with their peers, library leaders learn to recognize learning as a social responsibility.[1]

Building Relationships with Stakeholders

Through participating in library leadership, learners quickly understand the importance of professionalism and courtesy, realizing they represent their educators, peers, and school. While scanning books for an educator who wanted to use them in her classroom, one of Dione's elementary library leaders commented on her love for the book selected and her belief that the educator's learners would love it as well. She then thanked the educator for coming into the school library and wished her a good day.

Following the interaction, the educator made a beeline to Dione to remark how impressed she was with the professionalism and customer service skills she experienced in the school library. Reading widely and deeply enabled this library leader to share her positive opinion on the book while facilitating the school library's ability to build "strong relationships with stakeholders."[2]

Library Leaders Save the Day

Training and working with capable, interested, and independent library leaders to host a school event in the library presents a valuable opportunity to build relationships with those learners. When the school library hosted a meeting for the district professional organization, Broward County Association of Media Specialists (BCAMS), Diana volunteered to present a program on makerspaces in the high school. Library leaders had a clear knowledge of what was expected of them and began helping to prepare for their special guests. Learners were each assigned an area of the makerspace center that they were responsible for showcasing, speaking to the activity there and answering questions from the district school librarians.

Days before the event, Diana had an unfortunate accident that required her to have hand surgery the day of the meeting. Because of her preplanning and training with the learners, the meeting proceeded, highlighting the makerspace center as well as the library leadership program. Although Diana was still recovering from the surgery, she made an appearance at the meeting and was proud to witness the abilities of her library leaders.

Leaders addressed the adults as a whole group; each spoke about what they do, from helping other learners and library users find and check out books to making buttons and Cricut cards in the makerspace. These leaders were shining brightly with confidence as they spoke about their interests and abilities. Their presentation was even better than Diana had hoped. One memorable new library leader spoke from the heart about how she feels the school library is the place for her to be and how much she looks forward to the atmosphere and helping others use the library.

Because these exceptional library leaders took ownership of the situation and ran the meeting flawlessly and professionally, the local organization of school librarians was able to continue with their monthly meeting and the learners gained practical skills by sharing their experience with an authentic audience.[3]

An Avid Reader as a Teacher Assistant

It's a bonus when your library leaders are also avid readers. One library leader enjoyed discussing books and selecting new books for the high school library. As this individual aspired to work with people and in the health field, Diana gave her the opportunity to lead an English class in selecting books. She was a natural as she talked about various books and topics the learners might enjoy. This leader graduated this year, and Diana wrote in her yearbook, "Remember when you taught my class?" Learners inspire us, and they inspire and help each other. This individual was already reading widely and deeply, but in this leadership role, she was also able to exercise her competency across the Domains in the Curate Shared Foundation.[4]

Library Leaders Guide Their Peers

Library leaders can handle tasks during their designated class time, such as helping with checking in returned books, teaching new learners how to use a shelf marker, showing other learners where a favorite book or genre is shelved, and checking out books. When these young people take the reins and perform their tasks, it's important to let them know how much they are valued.

During a third-grade class period, some of the new trainees for Media TOTs in Dione's elementary school asked if they could assist with the circulation desk. Of course the offer was enthusiastically accepted, as it gave the young leaders an opportunity to practice their skills. Media TOTs were receiving praise for their customer service skills and knowledge of the school library management system on the computer, so the learners' classmates also wanted to be a part of the library team, often asking if they could help put the returned books back on the trolly or use the computer themselves to check out books.

Watching the Media TOTs perform tasks, the other learners wanted to emulate their success. "That's exactly right! You put the book on the Graphic Novel trolly. Great job!" one leader praised their classmate. How fulfilling to witness these young people building self-efficacy in their peers. Library leadership naturally creates scaffolding in the enactment of learning-group roles,[5] enabling opportunities for learners to work with others, build respect, and understand learning as a social responsibility.

Other Leadership Groups

Do you run your school's live news broadcast? Have the morning news crew arrive before school to create and rehearse their live broadcast at the start of the day. These leaders also need the same level of training as library leaders. Use the leadership tools taught in this book to train and promote these leaders effectively. Dione's ITE News Crew is led by the three learner directors who run the NewTek TriCaster live broadcast system, the soundboard and microphone, and the computer graphics via the laptop computer. In addition, these fifth-grade leaders maintain the professional integrity of the newsroom by supporting the rotating fifth-grade class anchors. Keeping the anchors on task while dealing with educator requests is no small feat. These learner leaders know they have Dione's full support and respect, and it shows in their work. When Dione needs to be out of the school for a conference or other absence, she knows the show will go on, thanks to her remarkable news crew. The atmosphere of the newsroom and the community of the crew is clearly one that promotes respect, and one in which learners feel empowered.[6]

Tout Your Success

Celebrate and share each step you take to enhance your school library program with your school community and stakeholders. How else will they know all the amazing things you are doing to support your school through your library leadership program? Many school librarians are leery about tooting their own horn. However, if not you, then who? Angie Thomas, author of *The Hate U Give*, spoke at the 2019 Florida Association of Media in Education (FAME) annual conference: "If we don't share our stories, then someone else will make up your story, and it may not be the story you want to share." This quote stuck with Dione and has given her the confidence to broadcast her accomplishments in the school library to her community, her peers, and her colleagues.

ACKNOWLEDGING LIBRARY LEADERS

With all the efforts that library leaders give to the school library program, it's imperative to show appreciation and gratitude for their hard work. Although some middle and high school leaders may earn service hours for volunteering or working in the school library, many serve the needs of library users without regard to being rewarded. Take time to offer sincere thanks and perhaps a small token of appreciation.

- Write a thank-you note to leaders for going above and beyond.
- Submit their names for school recognition or district awards.
- Have a visible compliments board, area, or box.
- Get a cake to celebrate leaders' birthdays during the months of that semester.
- During a holiday or monthly celebration, serve cookies or another treat.
- During a monthly celebration, feature artists, literature, and foods relating to the culture being celebrated, and have library leaders enter into a raffle for a gift card to a local business. Create an award certificate.
- Fill a basket with portable popular snacks and offer to leaders afterward.
- Provide bags of popcorn or other treats for leaders to take for a snack.
- Create buttons for Library Leaders of the Month.

Not every learner craves praise. One of Diana's library leaders, a gentle giant, often showed kindness to the school library visitors. Without prompting, he would ask if the guest needed help with their bags, boxes, or carts and offered to walk them to the elevator. Noticing this leader's compassionate nature and willingness to go above and beyond to assist and support the school library, Diana submitted his name to the Eagle Recognition program at school. He was so appreciative of the nomination that he didn't even need to win or be called for a prize for the boost in his confidence from this compliment to be visible.

Putting It into Perspective

The materials are here for you to build your beautiful school library leadership program. Take the first steps in constructing a realistic structure that can be improved upon year after year. Garner the support needed to strengthen your learners into thriving leaders. Take a realistic assessment of the strengths and weaknesses of your program and build in your own practical applications while showering your learners with thanks and praise. Relish your hard work, share in your successes, and stand back to marvel at all you have built.

NOTES

1. AASL American Association of School Librarians, *National School Library Standards for Learners, School Librarians, and School Libraries,* 2nd ed. (American Library Association, 2026), Learner III.D.2.: "Recognizing learning as a social responsibility."
2. AASL, *National School Library Standards,* School Library V.C.3.: "Building and advocating for strong relationships with stakeholders who recognize and support an effective school library."
3. AASL, *National School Library Standards,* Learner I.C.4.: "Sharing products with an authentic audience."
4. AASL, *National School Library Standards,* Curate Key Commitment: "Make meaning for oneself and others by collecting, organizing, and sharing resources of personal relevance."
5. AASL, *National School Library Standards,* School Librarian III.A.2.: "Scaffolding enactment of learning-group roles to enable the development of new understandings within a group."
6. AASL, *National School Library Standards,* Learner II.D.1.: "Creating an atmosphere in which learners feel empowered and interactions are learner-initiated."

PART II

Forms, Templates, and Essential Tools

These ready-to-use forms, templates, and tools are designed to help you quickly elevate your efforts to take students from learners to leaders who support their school library and learning community. To download these supplementary materials and customize them to meet the unique needs of your school library and learning community, visit **alaeditions.org/AASLextras.**

SAMPLE A

Call for Volunteers Poster

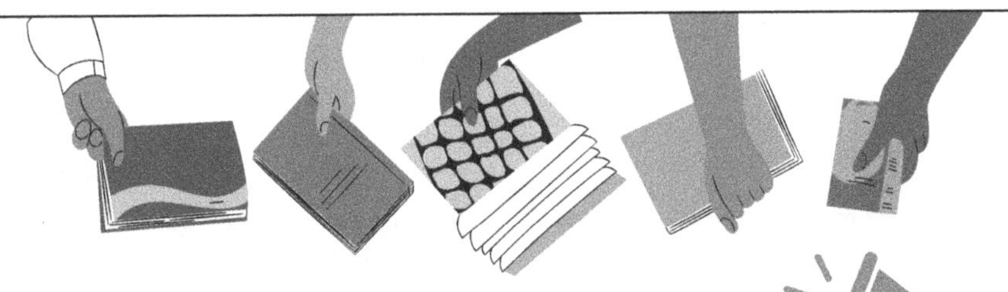

CALL FOR School Library Helpers

Do you love helping others?

Do you love books?

Are you willing to come before school to work with other amazing people?

School library helpers assist with:

- shelving books
- running the circulation desk
- managing the makerspace
- helping library users with requests

Location:
[Your school library]

GET SERVICE HOURS!

DEADLINE TO APPLY: [Date]

If interested, contact your school librarian for more information.

[Link to sign up]

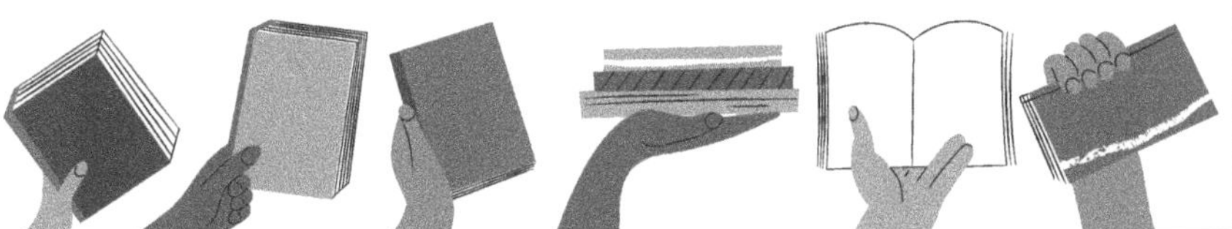

SAMPLE B

Library Leader Interest Form

Complete this form to share with the school librarian. Interest forms are due on ***[date]***. Please use the back of this form for additional space to write your answers.

1. First and last name:	
2. Classroom teacher/study hall period	**3. When would you be able to assist in the school library?** *Please select **only one** option.* ❑ After school ❑ During study hall ❑ Before school ❑ During lunch
4. Why do you want to work in the school library?	**5. What qualities make you a good library leader?**
6. What books do you like to read?	**7. What are your hobbies?**

8. Parent contact information

Parent name:

Parent phone:

Parent email:

SAMPLE C

Library Leader Interview Checklist

Interview Questions

- ❑ Why do you want to be a library leader?
- ❑ Have you ever helped in a library before?
- ❑ What area of the library are you most familiar with and look forward to helping?
- ❑ Are you tech-savvy?
- ❑ What is your favorite genre/type of book?
- ❑ Will you be looking to earn service hours?
- ❑ Name an educator who will provide a reference for you.
- ❑ Are you able to arrive on time? How will you get here?
- ❑ **[If this is an after-school program]** How will you get home?

First Impressions

- ❑ Learner is polite and engaged.
- ❑ Learner makes eye contact.
- ❑ Learner can converse well.
- ❑ Learner is an active listener.
- ❑ Learner works well with others.

Required Materials

- ❑ Permission forms turned in.
- ❑ Grades checked with classroom educators.
- ❑ Personal references checked with other educators.

Notes

❑ ______________________________

❑ ______________________________

❑ ______________________________

SAMPLE D

Library Leader Parent Information Letter

Dear Parent:

Your child has applied for a position as a student library leader at [***Your School Name***] for the ***[school year]*** academic year. Library leaders help shelve books, run errands, check-in books, set up the computers, manage the makerspace, assist other students in using iPads to take Accelerated Reader (AR) quizzes, and otherwise maintain the school library. Student library aides must meet the following criteria:

- Be enrolled in the fourth grade during the ***[school year]*** academic year.
- Arrive at school on time, seldom tardy.
- Practice regular attendance.
- Report to the school library by ***[time]***.
- Exhibit exemplary behavior.
- Complete tasks assigned.
- Return the Library Leader Permission Form and the Library Leader Behavior Contract to me by or before the first meeting. Our first meeting is ***[date and time]***.

Important Procedures

- Only library leaders will be allowed in the school library from ***[time]*** to ***[time]*** for library setup.
- Carefully read the Library Leader Behavior Contract with your child. If you and your child agree with the rules, please sign it. This contract must be signed to participate.
- Join the Library Leader Messaging App. This is the best way to keep in contact.

If you have any questions, please contact me at [***your email address here***].

[Your name and signature here.]

SAMPLE E

Library Leader Permission Form

Student's name:	Phone number:
Student's teacher:	Grade level:
Parent's name:	Parent's email:

Student's address:

My child is allergic to any food: YES NO (Circle one.)
If yes, what food(s)?

In case of emergency, I can be reached at:

In the event I cannot be reached, please contact:

Contact name:	Phone number:

By signing below, I agree to make the proper arrangements for my child to be dropped off promptly at 7:20 a.m.

I authorize my child to participate in Library Leaders at ***[your school's name]***. I understand and agree with the procedures of the club.

Parent or guardian signature **Date**

Optional: By signing below, I agree to allow my child to be videotaped for the purposes of booktalks and book reviews while participating in Library Leaders. I agree to allow my child's image to appear in school library promotional materials and any digital resources such as websites or blogs to promote the Library Leaders program.

Parent or guardian signature **Date**

Before using this sample, please ensure any waivers you create or plan to use go through your school library's approval channels and are approved by your institution's legal counsel.

SAMPLE F

Library Leader Behavior Contract

Student Name: **Teacher:**

Participating in the Library Leaders program is a privilege. The staff members who chaperone clubs volunteer their time to provide you with a safe environment to explore your interests, engage in leadership opportunities, expand your experiences at school, and have fun with friends. Signing this form means you understand and agree to follow the guidelines put in place to make club time safe and enjoyable for all. We want everyone to have fun in this club!

1. All school rules apply to any club activities.
2. Only respectful behavior toward adults and peers will be tolerated.
3. Attendance is mandatory, and you are responsible for keeping track of your club schedule.
4. You are part of a leadership club. Your fellow library leaders are counting on you to complete your part of the library duties. Your spot in the Library Leaders program may be revoked if you are hurting your fellow members by coming to club tardy and/or failing to work cooperatively to complete your assigned tasks.
5. You will try your best, keep a positive attitude, and support your fellow library leaders in the club.

Failure to comply with the rules will result in being removed from the club for the remainder of the year.

Student signature **Date**

Parent or guardian signature **Date**

SAMPLE G

Task Descriptions for Library Leader Roles

Job/roles	Task description
Check-in computer	Turn on the computer at the circulation desk and open our online system. Use the special circulation user name and password to log in. Click on circulation. Be sure to select "Check in" and then click inside the text box before scanning the barcode of the book being returned. Remember to greet your customers, look them in the eye and say, "Thank you!"
Put returned books on trollies	Help the circulation desk by placing the returned books from the book trollies to their respective shelves or bins. Help school library users who need their book incentive/brag tags. Always offer a smile.
Door greeter	Stand at the double-door entrance and greet each school library user warmly. Remember, our doors open promptly at 7:30 a.m.
Shelf straightener/ book displays	Go to each section of the school library and look for blank spaces on the shelves that need a forward-facing book. Use the bookends to straighten books that are falling over. Look for high-use areas that need special care.
iPads for AR helper	Gather the iPads from the labeled bins in the school library office. Set up a table for your station. Have all iPads turned on and ready for library users. Direct learners to log in to their school learning management system, and guide them in using Accelerated Reader (AR) appropriately. At the end of the session, verify all learners have logged out and place the iPads back into the labeled bins in the school library office. Remember to encourage and support your peers with a smile.
Makerspace/ Lego Room monitor	Open the Makerspace/Lego Room. Set out the centers you would like to have open that day. As makerspace users come in, greet them with a smile and ask if any assistance is needed. Walk around the room and offer help and encouragement. At the end of the session, remind users to help clean up their area. Put all centers back and check that the area is clean. Usher last-minute stragglers to the exit with a smile.

(continued on page 80)

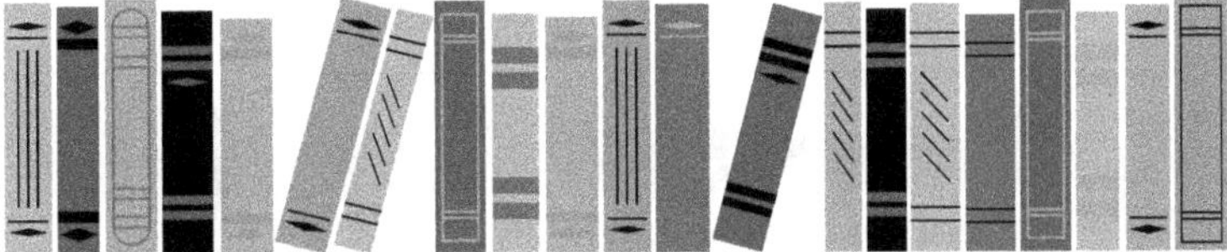

SAMPLE G

Task Descriptions for Library Leader Roles (*cont'd*)

Job/roles	Task description
Shelve books: "B for Biography" bin	Take the "B for Biography" bin to the biography section of the school library. Using the call number, place each book back on its correct shelf next to the other books about that same person. Remember to always use alphabetical order when placing books back on the shelf. Look for other books already on the shelf that have been mis-shelved and need to be relocated.
Shelve books: "E for Everybody" fiction trolly	Wheel the "E for Everybody" trolly to the E section of the school library. Using the call number, place each book back on its correct shelf next to the other books by that same author. Remember to always use alphabetical order when placing books back on the shelf. Look for other books already on the shelf that have been mis-shelved and need to be relocated.
Shelve books: 100, 200, and 300 nonfiction	Wheel the nonfiction book trolly to the nonfiction section of the school library. Using the call number, place each book back on its correct shelf next to the other books about that same subject. Remember to always use the Dewey Decimal Classification system's numerical order when placing books back on the shelf. Look for other books already on the shelf that have been mis-shelved and need to be relocated.
Shelve books: 500 nonfiction	Wheel the nonfiction book trolly to the nonfiction section of the school library. Using the call number, place each book back on its correct shelf next to the other books about that same subject. Remember to always use the Dewey Decimal Classification system's numerical order when placing books back on the shelf. Look for other books already on the shelf that have been mis-shelved and need to be relocated.
Check-out computer	Turn on the computer at the circulation desk and open our online system. Use the special circulation user name and password to log in. Click on circulation. Be sure to select "Check out" and then click inside the text box and enter the library user's name before scanning the barcode of the book being selected. Remember to greet your customers, look them in the eye, and say, "Thank you!"
Special projects	Ask the school librarian for the day's special projects, such as: taking books to an educator's classroom, stamping new books with the school logo, unpacking new boxes of books, helping to decorate tables with new displays, scanning books for inventory.

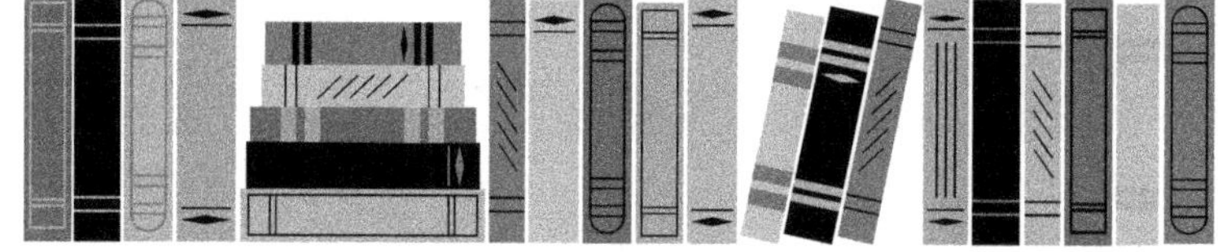

SAMPLE H

Library Leader Sign-In Sheet

We recommend using and updating this sign-in sheet weekly, so that leaders get an opportunity to explore all different roles and have consistency each week to learn each task. This allows leaders to have the same job for an entire week, ensuring time to practice and become familiar with a task. Each week, the names shift down one line, and they are assigned a new task to learn and can ask the previous week's leader any questions. Every day, the leader should initial the sign-in sheet in the day's column, put on their Media TOT badge, and begin their task.

Leader	Job/roles	M	Tu	W	Th	F
	Check-in computer					
	Put returned books on carts at the circulation desk					
	Door greeter					
	Shelf straightening/book displays					
	iPads for AR helper					
	Makerspace/Lego Room monitor					
	Shelve books: "B for Biography" bin					
	Shelve books: "E for Everybody" fiction carts					
	Shelve books: 100, 200, and 300 nonfiction					
	Shelve books: 500 nonfiction					
	Makerspace/Lego Room monitor					
	Check-out computer					
	Special projects					

THANK YOU!

- Turn ON library computers.
- Help library users research or find their book's call numbers.
- Please help shelve all books BEFORE the doors open to all students at 7:30 a.m.

Library Leader Skills Checklist

This checklist outlines the skills needed to be an effective library leader. Use it to guide your own learning and to help other leaders and library users.

To complete your training, this list must be verified and initialed by the school librarian.

Name: ______________________ **Class period:** ______________________

- ❑ attended the Library Leaders training

Basics: Interacting with School Library Users

- ❑ rules and procedures
- ❑ greeting visitors and checking passes
- ❑ answering the phone and taking a message if needed

Basics: Helping Users Find Resources in Our Collection

- ❑ finding a book using the school library's digital catalog tools
- ❑ locating a book on the shelf
- ❑ finding subgenres in fiction
- ❑ reading books, reading reviews, and knowing how to recommend a book to a library user
- ❑ book check-in and check-out
- ❑ understanding how the school library categorizes its books

Learning/Using/Teaching Technology

- ❑ printing documents at the school library printers/copiers
- ❑ making copies in the back room for educators and library staff
- ❑ logging on to computers (helping others too)
- ❑ using production resources, such as laminators and paper trimmers, die-cuts, and scantrons
- ❑ using interactive whiteboards (how to use and connect a laptop with a cord and wirelessly)

Using the Apps and Programs

- ❑ logging in to our school's "Single Sign-On" information portal and helping others who are having trouble
- ❑ logging in to the apps found in our school's "Single Sign-On" information portal
- ❑ navigating and locating information needed on our school website

Information Literacy/Teaching Research databases

- ❑ knowing where to locate our school's information databases and online encyclopedia

Social Media

- ❑ creating and suggesting content for school library social media accounts

Reading

- ❑ reading during every class period
- ❑ recording the time you spend reading in our school's reading incentive system

STEAM Center/Makerspace

- ❑ setting up a station you are interested in
- ❑ Describe your steps below for other learners to use:

____

____

____

Free Choice

- ❑ improving an area of our school library: STEAM, Quiet room, book displays, bulletin boards
- ❑ What area? ______________________________

  What did you do?___________________________

SAMPLE J

Library Leader Reflection Rubric

	Use this rubric with each learner in the Library Leaders program.				
	Unsure what to do 1	**Needs reminders 2**	**Follows instructions 3**	**Ready to lead 4**	**Score**
Respectful: Kind and eager to assist					
Communication: Able to speak to other learners and adults					
Collaboration: Works well with others					
Time manage-ment and fol-low-through: Completes tasks and cleans-up after self					
Problem solver: Attempts to come up with solutions to problems					
TOTAL SCORE List areas of strength and areas for improvement below.					

SAMPLE K

Recommended Reads Form

BOOK RECOMMENDATION

Title: ____________________

Author: ____________________

Star Rating

☆ ☆ ☆ ☆ ☆

A standout moment or character that made an impression:

Would you recommend this book to a friend?

Would you read this book again?

YES NO

This review was completed by:

BIBLIOGRAPHY

AASL American Association of School Librarians. *National School Library Standards for Learners, School Librarians, and School Libraries*, 2nd ed. American Library Association, 2026.

_____. "Common Beliefs." National School Library Standards, 2018. standards.aasl.org/beliefs.

Angelou, Maya. *I Know Why the Caged Bird Sings*. Random House, 1969.

Blanchard, Kenneth H., and Spencer Johnson. *The New One Minute Manager*. William Morrow, 2015.

Personnel Perspective. "The 80/20 Rule: Understanding Why 20% of the Workforce Does 80% of the Work." January 19, 2024. personnelperspective.com/2024/01/19/the-80-20-rule-understanding-why-20-of-the-workforce-does-80-of-the-work.

INDEX